Amazing but True
Bird Tales

Other Books by Allan Zullo and Mara Bovsun

Mews Items

Amazing but True Fishing Tales

Amazing but True
Bird Tales

Allan Zullo and Mara Bovsun

**Andrews McMeel
Publishing**

Kansas City

05 06 07 08 09 TNS 10 9 8 7 6 5 4 3 2 1

ISBN–13: 978-07407-5497-5
ISBN–10: 0-7407-5497-1

Library of Congress Control Number: 2005922475

www.andrewsmcmeel.com

To Renee, Jenna, Dylan, and Greg—
birds of a feather
— Allan Zullo

To Michael and Jay—two very rare birds
— Mara Bovsun

Contents

Amazing but True
Bird Tales

For the Birds

Introduction

BIRDS HAVE FASCINATED LOVERS OF NATURE for thousands of years. Sixteenth-century Scottish poet Bishop Gavin Douglas called birds "Dame Nature's minstrels." Because of birds, wrote nineteenth-century English writer Fanny Kemble, "carols of gladness ring from every tree."

We watch them through our kitchen windows and

binoculars. We welcome them with our bird feeders and birdbaths. Some of us breed them or race them. Some of us keep them as pets or shoot them—but only with cameras.

There are more than 8,600 species of birds spread throughout every corner of the world. They inhabit the busiest cities and the remotest woodlands; the coldest tundra and the hottest jungles; the wettest rainforests and the driest deserts; the highest mountains and the flattest prairies. They sing, warble, caw, wail, croak, chatter, shriek, quack, squeal, bleat, cluck, crow, grunt, whoop, hoot, honk, whistle, coo, chirp, cackle, tweet, screech, twitter, trill, squawk, and squeak. They range in size from the nine-foot-tall ostrich to the two-inch-long bee hummingbird. They can fly for thousands of miles like the Arctic tern, or not fly at all, like the emu. They can be as dull as a house wren or as colorful as a Catalina macaw.

For the Birds

This book is a celebration of wild birds and pet birds whose antics and adventures have astounded and amused bird lovers the world over. In the following pages, you'll read a collection of amazing but true stories about these marvelous winged creatures, including:

- The wild duck that flew with a cat on its back

- The crows that turned into arsonists

- The pet parrot that testified in court

- The injured seagull that sought help in a hospital

- The beer-swilling magpie that was banned from a pub

- The pigeon that thwarted a crook

- The wayward Hawaiian booby that ended up in Alaska

3

Whether they are magnificent birds of prey or sweet songbirds, exotic tropical pets or common backyard visitors, birds continue to captivate us. Perhaps it's because they symbolize not only nature's diversity in all its glory but also the one common yearning that all humans share—to be as free as a bird.

Flying Circus

Silly Birds

ON THE CATTLE RANCH OF MARLIN NEIDHARDT near Richardton, North Dakota, a mallard did something that perhaps no other waterfowl had ever done before—flew with a cat on its back!

It happened one unforgettable fall evening in 1986 when Neidhardt set out across the pasture with his cattle dogs Dingo and Penny and his pet tabby Kitty Boy.

Neidhardt wanted to check on a cow that he had rescued earlier in the day after it had fallen into a pond next to a dammed-up lake. As the foursome neared the dam, they spotted a flock of mallards resting by the edge of the water.

"Before I knew it, Kitty Boy had sprung for the mallards," Neidhardt recalled. "He spread all four of his legs as he dove after them. When he hit dead-center of the flock, they all took flight. There was an awful explosion of quacking and flapping wings."

One of the birds was furiously beating its wings but getting nowhere fast. Finally, like an overloaded cargo plane, it slowly got airborne and veered out over the lake about four feet above the water. "I didn't realize what I was seeing at first," said Neidhardt. "I saw the duck listing and then I heard a meow."

That's when he saw a sight that he could never have imagined possible: There, clutching firmly to the back of the flying duck, was Kitty Boy!

"That cat was square on the duck's back, scared silly. He had wrapped his forelegs around the duck's neck in a death grip. I couldn't believe it."

The flustered duck was just as scared. The frantic bird kept flapping its wings in a desperate attempt to gain more altitude while the panic-stricken Kitty Boy wanted down. The duck turned around and made a low pass near the dam where Neidhardt, Dingo, and Penny kept watching in disbelief.

Suddenly Dingo leaped up and knocked the mallard out of the air. The duck crashed into a stand of tall grass while Kitty Boy jumped off and scrambled under a bush where he tried to regain his composure. The shaken mallard took off again, this time without its heavy load, and flew away in the evening sky, having established an aviation record in duckdom.

When the world's first feline duck-rider emerged from the bush, Neidhardt wondered whether anyone would believe what he had just witnessed. The rancher recalled, "All I could think about was, 'How do I tell my wife that Kitty Boy flew on the back of a duck?'"

A blue jay had a nutty experience when it tried to steal some squirrel food.

George Peters, of Mt. Pleasant, Michigan, put leftover mixed nuts out for the squirrels. He spread the nuts on a bench on his deck, sorting them by size. George and his wife Barbara then sat inside by the window to see what would happen.

Moments later, a blue jay spotted the nuts and zeroed in on a peanut. The bird picked up the peanut in its bill and flew over the Peters' garden and dropped it. The jay made another trip to the buffet for an almond, then a filbert, then a pecan. The larger Brazil nut was a challenge, and it took a few minutes before the bird got it in its beak.

But the real fun began when the jay returned for the biggest nut—a walnut. "The bird tried to pick the nut up with its bill every which way to no avail," recalled Barbara in *Birds & Blooms* magazine. "Finally, it stepped back and, using its head as a battering ram, speared the nut with its bill. That's when its troubles really began. It tried flying up to our porch railing, but its head kept leaning over. Persistence paid off, however, and the bird finally made it to the railing."

Unfortunately, with its head weighted down by the speared walnut, the jay pitched over the railing and slammed headfirst into the ground. Not being able to walk with the nut on its bill, the jay laid its head on the ground and tried to dislodge the nut. Eventually, it succeeded. But the bird wasn't through with the walnut.

"The jay walked around the nut, eyeing it closely," said Barbara. "After a minute, it picked up a small twig with some leaves and covered the nut. After parading around the nut while cocking its head, the jay retrieved another leafy twig and did the same thing. Then it flew away. The whole scenario was unbelievable!"

Girls aren't the only ones who just want to have fun. Ravens do too, especially on windy and snowy days, according to birders on the chatline Birdchat.

"I always liked watching the ravens on windy days," said

Cathy Murrant, of Port Morien, Nova Scotia. "They gather at the cliffs and play on the updraft. I saw a raven doing this, only he took a hold of a treetop with his beak and held on. With his wings open, he just blew in the wind like a sheet on a clothesline—just like a raven windsock tied to the top of a tree . . . I thought it was quite funny."

A birder in Ketchikan, Alaska, reported seeing ravens do the same thing on windy days, but on her clothesline.

Ravens showed at least one bird-watcher how much fun they can have in the snow.

Birder Phil Schempf of Juneau, Alaska, recalled the time he watched ravens playing on a steep bank behind a local discount store. The bank was about thirty feet high and covered in snow. Many of the ravens were enjoying the delicacies in the store's Dumpster, which sat on top of the bank. But then they did something that totally surprised and amused Schempf.

"In no particular order, the ravens would individually tumble down the snowbank, usually rolling sideways rather than sliding head or tail first. The snow was deep, at least for a raven's legs, but they would hike back to the top of the bank for another go at it. I suppose they could have been removing parasites or involved in some intricate method of thermoregulation [regulating body temperature], but when my four-year-old does the same thing, I say she's playing."

When it comes to building nests, birds are great innovators for using whatever is available, as June Cook and her old black Labrador discovered.

The dog, named Miss Jessie, enjoyed the simple things

in life, like sunning under the bird feeder. Her coat had lost its luster and her fur could easily be pulled out.

"Most of the time, her feathered friends didn't pay attention to her," recalled Cook, of Rocheport, Missouri. "But one morning, I looked out the window to see a very busy tufted titmouse building a nest.

"Lo and behold, the bird would fly down to Jessie and pull out a bit of fur for the nest—and our canine Sleeping Beauty wouldn't even flinch. That titmouse had the softest, warmest nest in the neighborhood."

A tufted titmouse thought that a birder's hair made perfect nesting material.

Marion Dobbs, of Rome, Georgia, had gone to Cheaha State Park in eastern Alabama in 2002 to search for the state's first recorded Clark's nutcracker—a large, gray songbird found in the high mountain regions of the American West. She was able to locate the bird almost immediately. After observing it for a long period and taking photographs, Dobbs sat down at a picnic table to repack her belongings.

A tufted titmouse that had had been eyeing Dobbs for quite a while from a nearby tree trunk approached the woman. The bird unexpectedly perched atop Dobbs' head and proceeded to tug mightily at various strands of her hair.

"Obviously my windblown 'do' looked like a bonanza of nesting material—unless, surely not—she was foraging," Dobbs said in the chatline Birdchat. "This continued for maybe ninety seconds until I moved slightly. The bird departed, but soon returned and busied herself even more furiously, pecking and rummaging for a good purchase, sliding down first one side, then the other, departing again when I could stand the gnats no longer and took a swat.

"The behavior was repeated twice more for periods of several minutes each, not interrupted when I nodded regally to a carload of tourists, who hardly even slowed. I think, in fact, they probably sped up a little! I left several strands for the industrious little bird—only the gray, of course—when I finally had to depart with not a little regret."

When a rooster flew the coop, he chose an ironic place to roost—a Chick-fil-A restaurant.

Carlton Beall, manager of the fast-food chicken restaurant in Bluffton, South Carolina, said restaurant employees saw something "afowl" one summer morning in 2004 when the leghorn rooster walked inside and began strutting around the store's foyer.

"We let him out, but he kept hanging around," Beall told the *Carolina Morning News* of Beaufort, South Carolina. The employees nicknamed the rooster "Little Truett" in honor of Chick-fil-A's founder S. Truett Cathy and began feeding it biscuits, French fries, and cole slaw— but no chicken, of course. "It would have been gross to feed him his own kind," Beall said.

Brett Swanson, the restaurant's owner and operator, said a firefighter told him he saw the rooster crossing the road the day before. "We thought maybe someone would take him home," Swanson said. "He seemed friendly."

No one was sure how the bird got the strange idea to set up residence outside a place adorned with "Eat Mor Chickin" signs. Reporter Jennifer Moore wrote, "Several ideas have been suggested: maybe he's a University of South Carolina mascot [a gamecock] on vacation; maybe he lives in North Forest Beach and wanted to escape the tourists; or maybe he crows at customers to urge them to eat more beef."

The rooster made itself at home outside the restaurant for about a month and became a local celebrity. Occasionally he hung around a nearby Lowe's, but then he went missing for several days. A Chick-fil-A employee was so distraught he offered a reward of twenty chicken sandwiches to anyone who found and returned Little Truett alive.

The rooster eventually was found and taken to the Beaufort County Animal Shelter where director Susan Summerall arranged for the plucky clucker to live out the rest of his natural-born days on a farm. "He's not going to go to Kentucky Fried Chicken or anything," Summerall promised the newspaper.

During a vacation to Arches National Park in Utah, Martha Hill left a soda cracker on the ground and watched a raven pick it up and fly off to his cache. Next, she left two more crackers, then three, then four—and each time the raven returned, stacked them up, and carried them away in its bill.

"At five crackers, I thought the raven had met its challenge," recalled Hill, of La Grande, Oregon. "The growing crowd watched the bird place the crackers in a perfect stack of five. It tried to pick them up from several angles, but couldn't get them all in its bill. After a moment's hesitation, the raven ate one of the crackers, picked up the remaining four and flew off. We all cheered."

A female pheasant tried to lure a human male away from his bemused wife.

Hilary Goodfellow and his pregnant wife Denise were hiking with their dog near their home in Australia in the mid-1990s when they spotted a pheasant coucal perched on the power lines.

Sometimes known as a swamp pheasant, this common species is a large (twenty to thirty inches), clumsy bird with limited flying power and is indigenous to Australia's wetter northern and eastern coastal areas. It prefers life at ground level except when needing a perch to dry its rain-drenched feathers. Its trademark booming call—a repeated "oop oop oop oop" between the cock and the hen—carries for some distance, even over traffic noise.

During the Goodfellows' hike, a pheasant coucal was making its sound while staring directly at Hilary. As a lark, Denise suggested that Hilary imitate the call, which he did. "The bird immediately dropped to the ground and ran up to Hilary's feet, ignoring both me and our dog," Denise recalled in the chatline Birdchat. "It cocked its head on the side, looked Hilary in the eye, and then ran back to the bushes. Once there, it gave him a 'come hither' look. No such luck. So the coucal ran back to Hilary's feet, cocked its head at him again, and ran back, again to the bushes. Again Hilary resisted. The coucal pursued us for about seventy [yards]. On the way back it leapt out and tried again, pursuing us until we were nearly back to the car.

"Hilary said he resisted the temptation to desert me for

another, but only because he says the coucal was 'very ugly.' Let this be a warning to anyone contemplating marrying an English bird-watcher!"

A confused swan fell in love, but never found true happiness because the object of its affection was a swan-shaped pedal boat.

The male swan showed up at a boating pond in Hamburg, Germany, in 2002 and immediately fell head over webbed feet when it spotted one of the pond's pedal boats. For nearly two years, the swan refused to leave. In fact, it became so jealous that it chased off anyone who tried to take that particular boat out on the lake.

"At first we thought it was very funny," Amin Silwar,

owner of the rental boat company, told reporters in 2003. "But when we realized the swan wouldn't allow people near the boat, it wasn't so funny. I have lost a lot of business, but then again people are coming from all around to see the swan and his true love.

"I'm told swans choose partners for life, but I hope he finds a real mate eventually. We'll have to wait and see."

In the bird world's real-life equivalent to the movie *Fatal Attraction*, a large wild emu fell in love with a man and stalked him for days.

"It was mating season and she took a fond liking to him," said Diane Roberts, of the Animal Rescue Foundation of Mobile, Alabama. "She was absolutely intent that this was her mate."

The six-foot-tall, 150-pound bird showed up one day in 1998 at the rural home of Ed and Ann Stuardi of Mobile. It began drinking from a birdbath and eating berries off of bushes in their yard. Because it isn't every day that a wild emu shows up in your backyard, Ed was amused and fed the bird some dog food, that it quickly gobbled up.

But Stuardi soon realized that no good deed goes unpunished.

The bird stayed in the area for several days and began following Stuardi around whenever he stepped outside. Then it became aggressive and started chasing his cats. Stuardi, who was shorter than the emu, tried to frighten the big bird away by shooting his gun in the air. The emu just stood there, looking at him forlornly, according to the Reuters News Service.

Soon the emu was making noises deep in its throat, a mating call that Stuardi failed to recognize. The bird kept trying to approach him, forcing Stuardi to fend it off with a canoe paddle.

Finally, he couldn't stand the stalking any longer and called the sheriff's department. But the deputies didn't have the equipment to apprehend the winged stalker, so they summoned the Animal Rescue Foundation.

"Mr. Stuardi had been feeding her and when mating season hit, he almost got it," said Roberts. "He wasn't aware what the bird wanted or why she was stalking him. I've never seen one stalk a human with procreation in mind."

The animal rescue team had been looking for the bird for two months after members heard that a man who owned three emus had moved away from the area and abandoned them. When the team arrived at the Stuardi residence, it took several hours before members managed to corral the emu and get it into a horse trailer where it was taken to a farm that cares for injured wildlife.

Roberts said the emu's only injury was a broken heart. "Hopefully, she will meet another fellow and forget all about Mr. Stuardi. After all, he is a married man."

Helen was one of the most photographed and admired wild pelicans in the world. She was also one of the crankiest.

The white pelican lived for nearly thirty years at the Lake Merritt Wildlife Refuge in Oakland, California. In 1970, Helen, her mate Hector, and seven other half-grown pelicans were brought to the refuge by the California Fish and Wildlife Department. Helen and Hector were chosen to remain at the lake through a partial pinioning that kept them from full flight. Although the other pelicans eventually flew away, the couple remained behind to delight thousands of people through the years with photographic beauty and comical antics.

The pelicans lived on an island in the middle of the lake and were fed three pounds of smelt every day, but they added to their diet by scooping up lake herring on the side. The two lovebirds were devoted to each other and did everything together, especially their daily excursion around the lake.

But then in 1985 tragedy struck. Hector became entangled in a rope and drowned. Saddened bird lovers held a funeral service for Hector and buried him on the island. Helen was so devoted to Hector that every morning for the rest of her life, she stood sentry over his grave.

Helen grew ornery in her old age. In fact, she snapped at cars that drove past on the lakeshore road and she even bit a child's leg. Although she lived alone, she wasn't lonely, said naturalist Stephanie Benavidez. Helen often escorted wild white pelicans that happened to visit the lake. In her final years, a mute swan that wildlife workers named Lancelot earned her affection. But unlike Hector, Lancelot often disappeared for days at a time.

In 1999, Helen passed away. Bird lovers held a funeral for Helen, as they did for Hector, and buried her next to her true love. In announcing her death, the *San Francisco Chronicle* called Helen a "beloved, if somewhat crotchety, local character."

One winter morning in 1997, birder Julie Stielstra, of Lyons, Illinois, was on her deck filling the peanut tray when she heard someone vigorously shoveling snow nearby. But there was absolutely no one in sight. And although there were five inches of snow on the ground, it hadn't snowed in several days.

"The sound was very loud and very close, and since there had been no new snow, I wondered why anyone would be shoveling so energetically," Stielstra recalled in the chatline Birdchat. "Then I realized the sound was from overhead—and there was a starling sitting in my tree, happily pretending to be a snow shovel."

In the previous few weeks, there had been several significant snowfalls, so the starling had heard plenty of shoveling and scraping during that time—enough to learn to mimic the sound perfectly. "When I approximated the sound myself, it answered immediately in kind," said Stielstra. "I had heard they were terrific mimics, but this was the first time I'd heard it firsthand. It gave me a good chuckle on a cold, gray morning."

Stielstra said that because the starling was sitting outside her window imitating sounds, she was glad that it hadn't learned to mimic a snowblower.

A farm duck named Mr. Duck was sort of a quack. That's because his best friend was a beagle named Blackie.

The two were always together on the small farm of John Vrabely Sr. in Economy, Pennsylvania. It was a strange relationship, considering the fact that most beagles are known to hunt ducks.

But Blackie was a gentle soul who seemed to like all the

animals on the farm. So in 1998, when Blackie was nine years old, he didn't cause any trouble when the farmer was given six ducks. Unfortunately, over the next two years, all the ducks died except Mr. Duck.

Without his own kind to play with, the lonely Mr. Duck struck up a friendship with Blackie. The beagle was more than happy to be the pal and guardian of his new feathered buddy. They played in a nearby creek, shared the same food, and cuddled up with each other at night. Mr. Duck learned to stick close to Blackie for protection—especially when the duck stole food from the farm cats.

The dog and duck never wandered off the property, except on one weekend in 2002, when they failed to return home after being gone all day. Gerard Vrabely, who had inherited the farm following his father's death, began searching for the pair without success.

Later that night, a quarter mile away, teenager Jason

Kratochvil and his friends were out on the front porch of his home when they heard a quacking noise. That's when Blackie and Mr. Duck strolled into the yard.

Believing the animals were someone's pets and fearing for their safety on the dark streets at 11 p.m., Jason's mother Juanita decided the strange pair could stay. She herded the animals into her laundry room and fed them while her daughter, Nicole, called the police. The cops thought it was a prank. Come on, a dog and a duck? No one had reported them missing. After some convincing, the police took Nicole's name and number.

Meanwhile Mr. Duck, apparently bored with a steady diet of crackers, stuck his beak into Blackie's dish and ate some of his dog food. That night the duck slept with his head buried in the beagle's pepper-colored fur. "It's just so comical," Juanita told her family. "There really is a gentleness between them. They're a team."

The next day, Juanita phoned the *Beaver County Times*, the local newspaper, which published a story and photo about the dog and duck. Vrabely saw the article and immediately called Juanita.

"I never expected them to be here," Vrabely told her when he showed up to get the animals. Grinning, he added, "These are my bad kids. They're grounded."

When a pigeon on a New Zealand farm died, the lonely mate turned its affections to a new love—a sheepdog named Zoë. And they have been inseparable ever since.

Farmers Brian and Dorothy Richardson noticed a pair of pigeons living on their property and didn't think much about them and, in fact, didn't even know what breed the birds were. But in 2000, one of the pigeons died. Days later, the surviving mate began trying to make friends with the couple's sheepdog, who was then just a puppy.

Now, wherever the dog goes, the bird goes, Dorothy said in an interview with the New Zealand news organization *Stuff*. The pigeon doesn't have a formal name, but is known as Pretty Bird.

Even when Zoë is working the sheep in the paddock and in the fields, the bird is by her side. It then flies back to the house with the dog when she's done for the day. The pigeon sleeps in Zoë's kennel, and sits on the edge of her dish when she's eating. And whenever Zoë takes a nap, the bird likes to groom her. Zoë sometimes snoozes on the lawn with her paw resting on the bird, who lies quite contentedly under its weight.

Dorothy said passers-by often stop at the gate to watch the dog and bird wander around together. She said Zoë "talks" to the bird with a grunting noise, and the pigeon responds with birdcalls.

The unusual relationship has become an endless source of amusement, but there's one aspect of it that Dorothy doesn't find particularly funny. The dog is housebroken; the bird is not. "I am forever scrubbing the veranda," she said.

Hens and cats aren't supposed to get along. But rather than follow their instincts, fowl and feline sometimes follow their hearts.

In the early 1990s, a hen owned by Gloria Humphrey of Bristow, Oklahoma, often babysat for five kittens. Whenever the mother cat was off gallivanting, the hen would bring the kittens under her wing. She was very protective of "her" kittens, even to the point of fussing and pecking at the mother cat when she returned to nurse, bathe, and cuddle them.

When the kittens were old enough to run and play, the hen followed them around, clucking and fussing as if they were her chicks.

In a similar relationship, a mother hen and a mother cat formed their own cooperative family back in the early 1900s. Martha Wandell of Staten Island owned a Maltese cat and four kittens that lived in a roomy chicken coop with a hen that had eight chicks. The hen, the cat, and all their offspring got along just fine.

The cat protected the chicks from invading rats at night. Because the chicks tended to attract rats, the cat never went hungry and enjoyed fresh rodent dinners, to the advantage of her four young.

In the daytime, the cat accompanied the eight chicks and their mother on their daily walks. The feline acted as the fowl family's friend and guard. Learning from their mothers, the kittens and the chicks became best of pals.

A male flamingo at a nature reserve was so lonely and confused that he tried to incubate a pebble.

Andy, an Andean flamingo, spent more than two weeks sitting and warming a small stone that he thought was an egg, officials at the Wildfowl and Wetlands Trust in Gloucestershire, England, told BBC News Online in 2004.

Wardens at the reserve first assumed the bird had injured himself because he didn't want to move. But when the flamingo left to forage for food, it became obvious that the lonely bird wanted something to love.

Nigel Jarrett, a bird nesting expert, said male flamingoes "are very attentive and do make excellent fathers, but this is above and beyond the call of duty."

Jarrett eventually replaced the pebble with a fake

wooden flamingo egg. "We let Andy sit on the replica in case a female flamingo for some reason rejected her own egg," Jarrett explained. "We could have then placed the rejected egg under Andy for him to incubate as an alternative parent."

For more than two weeks, Andy dutifully tried to incubate the "egg," leaving it alone for only an hour a day when he went to feed.

Jarrett believed that Andy was intent on caring for the egg because the flamingo was still full of hormones at the end of the breeding season and didn't seem to have a mate. "It's possible that he did have a partner and for some reason their egg didn't survive because they can be snatched by gulls and crows," Jarrett said. "His mate may have left after the egg disappeared, but Andy may still not have noticed and carried on, thinking the pebble was a prospective chick."

Eventually Andy gave up his quest to hatch an egg and flew off.

For several years in the 1920s, a farmer's extraordinary rooster served as an alarm clock for people near New Rochelle, New York. What made the bird so unique was that it didn't crow—it whistled just like a traffic cop or basketball referee.

No one knew why the brown rooster could emit such a loud whistling sound. It used to crow, but then one morning it started whistling and never crowed again. No one really minded because people who lived near the old mill dam on Echo Lake enjoyed waking up to the sound of the whistling rooster. The bird was a local legend and made its owner, farmer Adam Sarnveld, proud.

But then one morning in 1926, Sarnveld and others woke up without hearing the rooster's daily whistle. When the farmer went to investigate, he discovered the bird had died.

Its death, though, solved the mystery of how the rooster could whistle so well. An autopsy revealed that years earlier the bird had swallowed a tiny metal whistle that had become lodged in its windpipe. Somehow, food was able to pass down the bird's gullet, but the whistle had remained stuck. Every time the rooster had tried to crow, it whistled instead. The bird died when a piece of food wedged in the lodged whistle, choking off its air supply.

Never again would the residents along Echo Lake wake up to the rooster's whistle.

A couple of starlings took a mailbox to receive their deliveries.

One day, Grace Preitz, of Ronkonkoma, Long Island, went out to her mailbox, the back of which rested against a large tree at a point where two low branches met. She opened it up to get her mail and was surprised to see a small nest inside. Because there were no eggs or birds close by, she carefully moved the nest to a cradlelike section of the tree right behind the mailbox.

"Two days later I was amazed to find that the two starlings that had built the nest had moved it back inside the mailbox," Preitz told the *New York Daily News*. What was equally surprising, she added, was that she then saw one of the starlings open the metal flap door on the mailbox.

Realizing that the birds were insisting on making the mailbox their home, Preitz didn't want to cause any further disturbance for them. She kept the metal flap door open and placed a plastic pail beneath the mailbox with a note to her mail carrier that read, "Mail here, nest above."

The starlings soon had some eggs that hatched—and the babies made their worldly debut by special delivery.

Dozens of rare birds were too lazy to migrate south for the winter, so they had to be driven there.

Ornithologists from the Konrad Lorenz Research Center in Gruenau, Austria, spent more than two years breeding the northern bald ibis species. The small ibis population, which had been widespread in Austria until it was nearly wiped out in the Middle Ages, lost its natural sense of orientation, an ornithologist explained.

In 2003, the birds were released with the expectation

that they would fly 500 miles to their winter quarters in the Maremma region in northern Italy. The birds, which average about thirty inches tall and have shiny black feathers, were expected to take between two and three weeks, depending on the weather, to make the journey.

Much to the chagrin of the researchers, the ibis refused to fly south. Some became disoriented and others just stayed around the research center.

Dr. Kurt Kotrschal, of the zoology department at Vienna University, said the birds were incapable of migrating south on their own because they were too spoiled and accustomed to being pampered. "The birds were used to the all-inclusive treatment at the research center," he told the BBC. "So we had to pack the lazy birds into the car and drive them."

Researchers decided that next time they would use ultralight planes to show the birds how to get to Italy.

Naughty Wild Birds

SEAGULLS WITH A CRAVING FOR ICE CREAM have been staging consume-and-zoom raids at Disney World for years, according to birders who witnessed the attacks.

The culprits are ring-billed gulls that knock ice cream cones out of the hands of visitors and then gobble up the treat within seconds before flying triumphantly away.

"Anyone who has fed the gulls on the coastal beaches in Florida is used to close encounters with pretty tame ring-bills, but I was unprepared for the behavior I witnessed at Disney World," said birder Dick Ferren, of Lenox, Massachusetts.

During a visit to the Magic Kingdom in Orlando, Ferren noticed several ring-bills perched on the roofs of various buildings near a canopied ice cream stand. "The folks would get the ice cream and walk out into the sun to discuss where to go next with their families," Ferren said in the chatline Birdchat.

"In the first 'attack,' a single ring-bill descended from the roof squarely on top of a man who was holding his ice cream cone slightly off to the side of his face while talking to someone else. He wasn't holding it up for the gulls. The gull had computed the situation, had surprised the man with a lightning descent upon the food, and had knocked it out of his hand. Immediately there were five or six gulls down on the ground running around . . . and in literally a twinkling of an eye, the once- or twice-licked ice cream had completely vanished, cone and all."

Ferren, who had a hunch that the gulls might be making a habit of surprising tourists, sat down under a nearby awning with his own ice cream cone to see how these gulls mugged the tourists. "In the next ten minutes I watched two other instances of theft of ice cream using a similar surprise attack," he said. "In all three instances, the gulls came directly down from the roofs at the elevated ice cream cones, and in each instance surprise and outrage was complete.

"The local Disney folks selling the ice cream were obviously aware of this chronic 'cleptoparasitism' and were issuing free replacement cones on request, which I thought was darned nice of them, considering that it was not their fault that the gulls had outwitted the tourists."

As a bird lover, Ferren said he was pleased that the gulls

showed off their smarts, even if it was for illicit gains. "It was intensely gratifying to see that for once, another species had demonstrated power over humans rather than the reverse."

Some of the Disney gulls have tastes for yummies other than ice cream. Greg Page, of Australia, said that while he was at Disney World, he had an encounter with a thieving seagull after buying a churro, a fried strip of dough sprinkled with sugar and cinnamon. "I took one bite and walked no more than ten paces from the churro stand when a big seagull swooped down, hit me on the head with its wing, took a bite of my churro, and then flew off."

Many visitors who have given online reviews of Disney World have mentioned avian ambushes. Among their comments: "Beware of those pesky seagulls if you sit outside." "The seagulls were awful while we were there." "If you eat anything outside, leave some for the gulls 'cause they're gonna take some of it anyway."

Two ornery birds—a hungry hawk and a screech owl—literally held up fishermen in two separate crimes.

The hawk proved to be a tough old bird that not only stole a fisherman's bait but also snatched his rod and reel. The victim was Tommy Meeks of Forest Park, Georgia, who had bought a new graphite rod and bait-casting reel with him to Florida's Orange Lake in 1980.

He should have stayed home. The bass weren't biting much that day because of cold, windy weather. The forlorn angler shivered as he cast out a large shiner, hoping for a largemouth bass. Then he put the rod down in the boat and breathed on his hands to stay warm. Suddenly, he looked up and saw a large hawk zeroing in on his bait. The bird went into its attack mode about ten feet above the water "with claws ready to grab my shiner on the surface," Meeks recalled.

The fisherman made a quick grab for his rod, but he wasn't quick enough. The hawk snatched the shiner and jerked the new rod and reel right out of the boat. "I was stunned," Meeks said. "At first the rod sank, but the hawk flew on and suddenly my fishing rod jumped out of the water like a big old bass."

Meeks couldn't believe what he was seeing—the hawk was flying off with the shiner and thirty feet of line trailing straight down to his rod and reel. The rod skipped along the surface of the lake, sometimes rising six feet in the air as the hawk struggled to make off with its prey.

Then Meeks snapped out of his astonishment and cranked up his outboard motor and took off in pursuit. He wanted his rod and reel back.

The hawk had a 200-yard head start on him, but Meeks

closed in on the bird, which by now had flown into a thick patch of lily pads. Each time that the rod fell into the water, the big bird would find another burst of strength and power up over the lily pads. Meeks ran his boat wide open into the weeds and caught up to the rod.

"I was just fixing to grab it when the hawk veered off and my rod slammed against my boat," he recalled. The line broke and the triumphant hawk continued on its way with the stolen shiner. Meanwhile, Meeks' new rod and reel sank out of sight in eight feet of water. "I better not ever see that darn hawk again," he said.

Pro bass angler Rhonda Wilcox felt the same way about a nasty screech owl she encountered while bass fishing with her father on Lake Fork in Texas in 1987.

Wilcox cast toward the bank and turned to her father to ask him a question when they heard a big splash in the water. Thinking she had a strike, Wilcox turned, reared back on her rod, and set the hook. To her complete surprise, her line went straight up in the air.

"This screech owl—big as a fat chicken—had swooped down and picked up my bait and was flying off with it," Wilcox recalled. "Incredibly, the owl wasn't even hooked. It was clutching my plug with her claws and wouldn't let go.

"I needed that bait because it was the only one like it that I had, so I started reeling in the screech owl. I was standing in the very front of the boat with ten rods all around me and I couldn't move. My daddy came up and grabbed the line about four feet below the owl."

Not about to give up that bait without a fight, the owl went on the attack. "It flew right at my face and I screamed bloody murder," Wilcox said. "I tripped over some of the rods on the deck and almost fell overboard. As the bird tried to take off, my daddy yanked on the line to bring the bird back and then he grabbed it with his hands."

While her dad held the bird, Wilcox pulled on the bait. But the screech owl still wouldn't give it up. The angler finally got a pair of pliers and had to pry the plug out of the owl's claws.

"Daddy then pitched the bird high in the air, and it flew up on a tree branch just seven or eight feet away," Wilcox said. "I could have reached up there and hit it with my rod, it was so close. The owl cocked its head and opened its eyes real wide like owls do, and it glared at us, as if to say, 'You fools. How dare you try to take my food away from me!'"

A bald eagle "shot down" a commercial jetliner.

It all started innocently enough in 1987 near Juneau, Alaska. The eagle dived down and snagged a salmon that was swimming peacefully in a river. The bird then flew off toward its aerie with the delectable fish clutched in its talons.

But the eagle spotted another giant bird heading straight for it—and the scaredy-cat eagle decided it was best to relinquish its prey and flee for its life. Talons flew open and the salmon fell through the air. The fish slammed into the cockpit window of the bigger bird—an Alaska Airlines Boeing 737 that had just taken off from Juneau. Fortunately, the window didn't break.

Still concerned about possible damage, the pilot of the Anchorage-bound jetliner made an emergency landing in Yakutat 200 miles away, where mechanics made a careful inspection. "They found a greasy spot with some scales, but no damage," said Paul Bowers, the Juneau airport manager.

The flight's forty passengers were forced to cool their heels for about an hour before the plane was pronounced airworthy and allowed to continue on to Anchorage.

Fowl-Ups

The bizarre incident went down in aviation history as the first-ever midair collision between a commercial jetliner and a fish. The eagle apparently escaped injury, but was no doubt keeping a vigilant eye on those bigger, noisier birds.

Birds have been known to steal golf balls, but nowhere is it more prevalent than at the Yellowknife Golf Club where an untold number of golfers have gone stark "raven" mad.

It's the only course in the world where birdies get their golfers about as often as golfers get their birdies. That's because eagle-sized ravens are notorious for swooping down from the trees and snatching golf balls right off the fairways.

Yellowknife is the northernmost course in the world, located just 250 miles south of the Arctic Circle in the

Northwest Territories, Canada. And although the nine-hole course is all sand spread out among rocks and evergreens, the golfers' major hazards are the ravens.

For some Poe-etic reason, the ravens of Yellowknife have been stealing golf balls—especially new, shiny, white ones—since 1950. The modus operandi is always the same. A raven usually perches on a tree about 200 yards away from a tee and waits for a drive to land. Then, ignoring the angry shouts of the golfer, the bird glides down to the ball, picks it up in its beak, and heads off to its stash.

The thefts have led to the adoption of a local rule. On the back of every Yellowknife scorecard, Rule 6 states, "No penalty assessed when ball carried off by raven."

Years ago, golfers brought along .22-caliber rifles or shotguns to scare or kill the ravens. But, according to accounts back then, the ladies of the community got up in a different sort of arms and demanded an immediate end to the sniping. They argued that ravens were the only birds remaining in the desolate area during long winter months, and the women were happy for any living company they could get.

Few of the birds were ever killed. "The ravens were either very cunning or our golfers were extremely poor shots," said longtime golfer George Inglis. "I've seen only one dead raven on the course. Someone had hung him from a fairway tree, possibly in an attempt to show the other ravens that crime doesn't pay."

But there has been no letup of these fowl deeds. In fact, the winged theft ring has become even bolder. On several occasions, a golfer has been robbed by the ravens of as many as six balls in a single round, according to club official Ed Cook.

There are two schools of thought about the ravens' motives: (1) The birds believe the balls are eggs and cart them off to their nests or roosting areas. (2) The birds hate golfers. That may explain why many ravens simply bury the balls in the sand elsewhere on the course. Most golfers believe the latter.

In recent years, ravens have been hiding their booty far from the course. Three miles away, hikers found a raven's nest crammed with seventy-eight balls.

"It seems a new game has developed between ravens to see which can steal the most balls," said Cook. "Within one week, two caches of balls were found on roofs of buildings in [the town of] Yellowknife. More than fifty were found on one roof, and on another high-rise building there were more than a hundred."

One victimized golfer suggested that members of the Yellowknife Golf Club be allowed to carry shotguns in their golf bags. The idea was rejected. But if golfers were armed, imagine what would happen to all the ball thieving. Quoth the raven, "Nevermore."

A mockingbird turned into a mass murderer—of butter-flies. It had gobbled hundreds of rare butterflies in a zoo exhibit over two weeks while evading capture.

In 2002, the wild bird apparently entered the Hilbert Conservatory at the Indianapolis Zoo through an open vent or window. The sixty-five-foot-high conservatory housed an exhibit of about 1,500 live butterflies—small creatures of beauty to visitors, but a smorgasbord of tasty treats to the mockingbird.

For two weeks, the bird gobbled hundreds of rare butter-flies while zoo employees tried to catch it so they could stop the carnage. "You can't blame the bird because he was doing what came naturally," zoo gardener Susan Micks told the

Indianapolis Star. "The joke was, we'd catch him eventually because he'd get too fat to fly."

As it dined on the butterflies, the mockingbird evaded capture by flying high and staying out of reach in the conservatory. The killings stopped after two weeks when zoo workers soaked the bird with a hose, stunning it just enough for them to catch it in a net.

According to zoo spokeswoman Judy Gagen, the mockingbird ate about $1,000 worth of butterflies. The bird took a special liking to brilliant neon butterflies called blue morphos, whose population was especially hard-hit. Gagen said the bird was removed from the conservatory and released "far, far away."

A bald eagle that apparently wanted to play football on the beach with children became so aggressive it had to be captured.

For nearly a week in 2001 at Hampton Beach State Park in New Hampshire, the eagle swooped down on people as they played football on the sand. During its time at the beach, the bird clawed three-year-old Kayla Finn as she was playing with two other children. Her father had to run and shoo the bird away as it made a grab for the child. She was scratched, but didn't require medical treatment after the incident. Two adults and another child were also slightly injured during the eagle's invasion.

Bemused beach-goers had reportedly encouraged the one-year-old bird by feeding it. "He associates people with food, and that's the worst possible situation for a wild bird," Peter MacKinnon, Hampton animal control officer, told reporters. The bird managed to avoid capture by ignoring wildlife officers' offerings of dead fish. Since the eagle was attracted to footballs, officials later tried to lure it close to them by tossing around a small green football. The eagle stayed out of the game.

Watching the failed attempts to capture the bird became the main source of amusement at the beach and drew huge crowds.

The bird was finally caught in a baited net by an animal control officer in Salisbury, Massachusetts, near the New Hampshire border and was taken to the local Coastal Animal Clinic. The eagle, which had a six-foot wingspan, was identified as a bird that had been released from a wildlife reserve in North Carolina. It was later set free in a remote area.

MacKinnon said, "Other beaches have sharks, but at Hampton, we had to be different. We had to get an attack eagle."

Birds, millions of them, were driving a small Maryland town cuckoo.

For months in 1974, millions of starlings, grackles, and blackbirds darkened the sky at sunset, scared dairy herds, destroyed cornfields, and created a health hazard for the bird-leaguered hamlet of Graceham. The roost, one of the largest ever seen, was estimated to contain about 10 million birds, outnumbering the town's 400 residents by 25,000 to one.

Graceham, located about ten miles from the presidential retreat of Camp David, apparently had such fine food and lodging for the migrating birds that they decided to roost there. Actually, most of them roosted in March in the pine trees of Edgar Emrich's sixty-acre farm. The birds polished off the remains of old corn stalks in his fields and then swooped in on a neighboring farm and pecked away at 600 pounds of grain intended for their turkeys.

The birds chased cattle from their feed troughs, dive-bombed barns, and ripped open bags of seed. The intruders forced farmers to change dinnertime for their cows to after dark—when the birds had finished gorging themselves for the day and had returned to Emrich's pines.

On rainy days, the birds swarmed beneath roof overhangs and onto porches. In some areas of Graceham, bird droppings were more than two inches deep. There were concerns that the droppings would bring a disease called histoplasmosis, which is caused by a fungus that feeds on the droppings and can be transmitted by air to animals and people. The birds even splattered houses and cars and dirtied laundry that had been drying on clotheslines.

Each evening the sky blackened and the birds erupted in a chorus of shrill whistles. "Our dog Herman shakes when they fly by," Clare Myers told UPI at the time. "They go into his doghouse, chase him out, and eat his food. It's unbelievable, it's frightening, but it's for real."

County health department official Paul Beale told reporters, "We're declaring war on them, but we don't want to kill any of them or we might leave ourselves open to an insect population."

Every evening officials fired flares, shotguns, firecrackers, and twenty-four small cannons that shot blanks. They set up loudspeakers and played tapes of calls of distressed birds, all to no avail. The townspeople were so desperate they even began blaring the soundtrack from Alfred Hitchcock's horror film *The Birds*, a tale of an avian attack on humanity. "We aren't going to upset these birds as much as they're upsetting us," sighed resident Roger Wiley.

Graceham didn't want to make the same mistake as officials in Fort Campbell, Kentucky, did when their town came under siege from a roost that was estimated to be 12 million strong. The birds destroyed $2.65 million worth of grain in the area and caused about twenty-five persons to come down with histoplasmosis. Officials there poisoned tens of thousands of birds, but that created other problems—such as an insect infestation, a horrible smell, and mounds of carcasses.

Adding to Graceham's woes, the town's dilemma drew national attention, which meant that hundreds of gawkers from bigger cities came to see the huge roost. The visitors irked residents by clogging the narrow country roads and parking on their lawns.

Some residents tried to take the invasion with a sense of humor and ran a contest to see who could come up with the silliest solution to get rid of the birds. One person suggested spraying the trees with yellow paint, saying "If nothing else, the birds will look at each other in disgust and fly away."

Another suggested putting 10,000 starving cats in the woods.

The birds finally dispersed, but not because of anything that people did; it was Mother Nature. The weather warmed up and the birds flew off.

In a standoff between a man and a big bird, bet on the one with the wings. A man in Australia tried to intimidate a large, flightless bird called a cassowary . . . and lost.

The cassowary is the largest bird in Australia and the second biggest in the world. (Only the ostrich is bigger.) This huge endangered bird, which lives in rainforests and swampy forests, can grow to over six feet tall and weigh about 130 pounds. It has powerful legs and three-toed feet with sharp claws, and protects itself by kicking. It can run up to 32 mph and jump five feet high. It is a formidable bird and not one that is easily bullied.

According to a 1998 article in *New Scientist* magazine, a district forester from Cairns, Australia, was on his way home when he rounded a bend in the countryside and saw a car parked in the middle of the road. He stopped and asked the driver if anything was wrong.

"That . . . that thing there! That's what did it!" shouted the enraged driver, pointing up the road to a six-foot-tall cassowary. The driver then explained that he was motoring down the highway when he encountered the large bird, which was standing in the middle of the road. After coming to a stop, the man spent a few minutes admiring the bird.

Then, wanting to get on with his trip, the driver tried edging his car forward, hoping to get the cassowary to move out of the way. The bird stood its ground, so the driver blew the horn. The cassowary strongly objected to this and landed a vicious kick that pushed the car's radiator back onto the fan, cutting a hole in it. The victorious cassowary then strutted triumphantly up the road, while coolant from the damaged radiator drained away.

As *New Scientist* put it, "Birds one, cars nil."

Two crows created havoc for several weeks in 2004 in a parking lot by stripping the rubber off of cars' windshield wipers.

Driver John Foster told BBC Online News he lost six sets of wiper blades after the avian culprits targeted his car in the Askham Bar Park and Ride parking lot in York, England. He said it took several weeks, and a few sets of new wiper blades on his Ford Mondeo, before he figured out what was happening.

"I got into the car one night and was driving home when I realized the rubber was coming off the passenger-side wiper," Foster said. "So I had the blades replaced and three weeks later the same thing happened again." He thought the blades were faulty and put new ones on, but after the third set, he knew something else was wrong.

A little sleuthing pointed to the two crows, who left a trail of evidence. "I was walking back to my car one evening and noticed four or so bits of rubber on the ground," Foster recalled. "So I went to the park and ride office and the guy said, 'Oh yes, we know about it. It's crows and we've got them on video.' I was staggered. I just couldn't believe it. I thought it was vandals."

Actually, they were birdbrained hooligans.

A spokesman for the Royal Society for the Protection of Birds (RSPB) had several theories to explain the birds' bizarre behavior. He said the birds could have been attracted by the taste of a component in the rubber. Another possibility was that the birds saw their reflections in the windshields and attacked the wiper blades, believing they were rival crows. Drivers were advised to wrap their wipers in towels or to coat their wipers with aluminum ammonium sulphate to keep the crows at bay.

Although the two birds were being a costly nuisance to the drivers who had to replace their wipers, many locals took a shine to the crows—and even gave them the names of Russell and Sheryl (presumably after actor Russell Crowe and singer Sheryl Crow). When word spread that officials planned to kill the feathered fiends, bird lovers protested. The City of York Council listened and issued a stay of execution for the crows. Officials agreed to catch Russell and Sheryl and move them to an area where they wouldn't get into any trouble.

Birds in Japan are turning into firebugs.

Crows and blackbirds were found to be responsible for starting a rash of fires near a holy shrine in Kyoto in 2002.

Officials thought an arsonist was trying to set fire to the Fushimi Inari Taisha Shrine. But security cameras caught the real culprits—crows and blackbirds were stealing lit candles that were hanging up around the property, according to the *Mainichi Daily News*. When the birds dropped the lit candles on piles of leaves near the shrine, they started the fires that had residents fearing an arsonist was on the loose.

"Crows love oily food, which is probably why they stole the wax candles," explained Hiroyoshi Higuchi, a Tokyo professor of ornithology.

Kyoto is not the only place in Japan where winged arsonists have been at work. Other fire-setting birds are jungle crows—huge, jet-black creatures with intimidating beaks, killer claws, and a caw that sounds like a seagull on steroids. They measure about two feet from beak to tail and sport a wingspan of more than a yard.

The crows have always been pests to farmers in the countryside. In 2002, a crow was blamed for a forest fire in Iwate prefecture in northern Japan. Workers had been burning bags of outdated potato chips at a garbage dump. A witness reported seeing a crow pick up a flaming potato chip bag and drop it over dry weeds, igniting the blaze.

A year earlier, there had been another case of suspected crow arson. A fire was sparked when a bird picked up incense from a graveyard and dropped it in a nearby forest. Crows flock around cemeteries, where food, including vegetables and fruit, is often brought as a gift for dead ancestors and where those paying respects often light incense sticks. "You cannot blame anybody for a crow-caused hazard," said Muneo Hishinuma, the fire chief in the city of Kamaishi. No, but you can blame the crow.

Crows took revenge on a fisherman who killed some of their own.

The agency India News reported that a young man named Ramanbhai was harassed for weeks by crows in his village of Itawad in the Vadodara district. He and other villagers believed that the avian attacks were in retaliation for his murder of several crows.

Ramanbhai who, like many in the area goes by a single name, said he dried fish by sunning them on his terrace, but the crows were devouring the catch. With his only means of income threatened, Ramanbhai sprinkled a poisonous liquid on the fish in 2004 and left them spread out for the crows to eat. Many of the crows that ate the poisoned fish died.

But that didn't end his troubles. In fact, it compounded them.

According to India News, the crows attacked Ramanbhai as soon as he stepped out of his home the next day. The attacks continued for several more days, even after he tried to appease them by leaving dead fish for them to eat. The crows were unimpressed with his act of contrition, and they continued to noisily swoop down on him whenever he left his home. In fact, the situation became so bad that Ramanbhai had been reduced to protecting his head with a pan every time he stepped outside.

When a crow began attacking pedestrians in a German town, police were called in to arrest the culprit. But the bird always managed to escape. However, the cops came up with a final spirited attempt that captured the crow—by getting it drunk.

Fowl-Ups

In 2003 in Dortmund, the crow inexplicably took a strong dislike to people walking into the park. One woman fell to the ground when the large black bird swooped down on her. A seven-year-old girl was also attacked. Other pedestrians were harassed by the winged menace.

Officers intent on apprehending the crow used cat food as bait. The crow took the bait, but flew off before it was caught.

After several attempts, officers decided to lace the food with schnapps. It worked. "After its excessive consumption of alcohol, the animal lost its sense of direction and could be caught," police said in a statement. "It is now sleeping off its hangover at a local animal protection charity."

A Japanese police officer recovered a stolen wallet by following a hunch that the thief was a crow.

A thirty-year-old woman had placed her wallet in the front basket of her rented bicycle and pedaled out to a quiet ocean-side vista in the Okinawan island of Hateruma in 2004. "The scene was the southernmost point of Japan—an open area on top of a hill," local police officer Tatsuyuki Ito told the news agency AFP. "The lady went there with a friend, but there was no one else in the area because the weather was bad on that day." The woman was enjoying the view for a few seconds and when she glanced back at her bike, she realized that her wallet was missing.

After receiving the report of a possible theft, Ito, a twenty-eight-year-old sergeant with six years experience on the force, immediately developed a hunch. "I bought bread on the way to the scene," he recalled. "I placed it on top of the monument [that marked the southernmost point of Japan]. I hid for a few minutes. As expected, crows came down and took the bread to a nearby screw-pine bush. I followed the birds until they settled down to eat the bread. That's where I found the red wallet. Crows did not eat it."

No charges were filed and the case was closed.

Pheasants don't like the color red and they don't like mail carriers—and they really, really don't like mail carriers in red vehicles.

This is especially true in the United Kingdom.

In 2004, a pheasant that took up residence in the village of Moylegrove, near Cardigan, west Wales, chased red vehicles

and pecked at people wearing red. It showed a particular dislike for postmen, attacking them as they emptied mail from
the red mailbox in the center of the tiny village.

"The bird seemed to know when it was 4 p.m. and
waited for the postman," said resident Jutta Greaves. "I
have seen it going for a postman as soon as he arrived. The
postman was in a red van, and the pheasant pecked his
hand and his arm as he was opening the box." She said she
had seen the pheasant peck at other postmen.

One of the mail carriers attacked by the pheasant was
Delano Thomas, who was followed on his deliveries by the
bird and then attacked as he tried to empty the mailbox. He
told the local newspaper the *Carmarthen Journal*: "At first, I
thought the pheasant was being friendly. But, as I unlocked
the box, he pecked the back of my hand. He got a size nine
boot for his trouble but he came back for more."

Fowl-Ups

It wasn't the first time that a west Wales village was harassed by a confrontational pheasant with a dislike for mail carriers. Postman Gerald Lloyd stopped deliveries to the village of Wiseman's Bridge near Tenby in 1999 because of a mean-tempered pheasant that the locals named Henry. Villagers were forced to make a fourteen-mile round trip to pick up their mail until a new postman was brought in.

But just days before Lloyd was due to return to his rounds, Henry was found mangled on the roadside. The killer has remained at large.

Royal Mail spokeswoman Val Bodden said at the time, "We were very sorry to hear about the sad demise of Henry the pheasant. But we deny all responsibility. We never wished him any harm.

"We've had all types of animals attacking our posties over the years, but it isn't often a postman is terrorized by a bird."

However, it seems pheasant attacks on posties are on the increase.

In 2004 near Devon, England, Jeffrey Patton, who heads the post office in the village of Swimbridge, was forced to ward off an angry pheasant on his daily rounds for several weeks. He told the BBC News Online he had been bitten and scratched by the bird. Not only that, but on one occasion the pheasant flew right into his van.

Patton said he thought the pheasant disliked him instantly because the mail van that he drove was red, and this infuriated the winged attacker. Every time Patton delivered mail to a particular farm, he was followed back down the lane by the pheasant. "He just doesn't like the red, I think," said the mail carrier. "As he sees the red of the van, immediately the hormones and aggression kick in and he's off."

Apparently, pheasants the world over don't like postmen in red vehicles.

In 2003 a Japanese mail carrier reported he was harassed by an angry pheasant, which chased and attacked him as he completed his rounds.

Mutsumi Oki said the cock bird lay in wait for him each day as he rode his red motorbike around the Yagitsure district of Myogi. Oki, thirty-eight, told the newspaper *Asahi Shimbun*, "The bird always scares me because whenever it sees me, it comes at me at full speed with such an aggressive look."

Keisuke Ueda, professor of ornithology at Rikkyo University, said the pheasant probably assumed Oki was a rival. "Male pheasants have a red hanging protrusion on their gullet," he explained. "About this time they become especially jittery because their breeding season starts from spring to summer. The bird might be reacting to the motorbike's red color, seeing it as a rival male, trespassing on his territory."

The blackbirds of a small English village learned how to imitate car alarms.

They mastered the alarming trick in 1996 after an individual bird suspected its territory was about to be invaded, explained David Hirst, a spokesman for the RSPB. The bird had incorporated the sound of the car alarm into its song, and it was taken up by dozens of other blackbirds in Guisborough, North Yorkshire, England, creating a daily dawn chorus that jolted residents from their sleep.

Bartender Donald O'Shea told reporters he discovered the phenomenon when he rushed out at dawn to confront what he thought was a car thief but found only a blackbird in mid-song.

Journalist Mark Topping had a similar experience. "I started hearing this irritating noise outside at 5 a.m. every day," he said. "It certainly seemed to be a car alarm, but there wasn't one close enough to be making such a row. Then I saw this one particular blackbird sitting in our alder tree, outside the bedroom window. It was giving its everything, but instead of the usual pleasant song of the blackbird, it was recreating the din made by a car alarm. After I heard that one bird, I began to realize others had picked it up as well."

The European blackbird—actually a thrush, a close cousin of the American robin—can imitate everything from a phone ringing to a cat meowing, said bird-watcher Liz Taylor (not the actress) who lived nearby. She said the blackbirds were enjoying a good joke at the expense of their sleeping human neighbors.

"When I lived in Bombay," Taylor said, "we had a trio

of large crows in our garden, one of which could imitate exactly—and in a Scots accent—my voice calling out for the gardener. When he arrived in response to my summons, they would jump up and down on the wall, cackling horribly."

Free-roaming peacocks were exiled from a Danish park after they attacked parked cars.

Officials in Copenhagen admitted in 2002 that they were getting inundated with complaints and claims for damages from motorists visiting Frederiksberg Park. Head gardener Soren Selch told the newspaper *Expressen* that the birds tended to strike at new cars or newly washed vehicles with their claws and beaks. He said the peacocks had nothing against the driver or the vehicle. It was just that the colorful birds were attacking their own reflection, thinking it was a rival. The park paid more than $10,000 in repairs and paint touch-ups for visitors' cars.

Bird lovers wanting to save the park's fifteen peacocks claimed the birds were a major attraction, and called on car owners to stop polishing their vehicles if they wanted to visit the park. But the birders' plea had the impact of a feather. Some of the more aggressive peacocks had to be put down while others were moved to a secret location on the island of Zealand.

In 2004, a buzzard that hated cyclists launched a series of attacks on them on a country road in Devon, England.

Over a period of a month, the bird struck more than two dozen cyclists, injuring several of them.

Linda Johnston, a member of the Devon branch of the Cyclists Touring Club, was on her bike one evening near the village of Holsworthy when she was struck on the back of the head by the buzzard. "It really hurt and gave me a fright," she told the BBC News Online. "After it hit me, I could see it hovering and thought it was going to come back, so I speeded up and got away as quick as I could. It is quite dangerous. It could make someone lose their balance and fall off."

Retired toolmaker Paul Dixon, seventy-one, secretary of the cycling club, was another victim of the buzzard. He wasn't wearing a helmet when the angry bird swooped down on him and clawed the top of his head, leaving him with blood pouring out of three deep scratches.

All twenty-two competitors in two long-distance cycle races were also attacked at the same spot two weeks earlier. The dive-bombing bird had struck other cyclists with such force it gouged holes in their helmets. The attacks forced a time trial and another scheduled bike ride to be rerouted the following week.

Experts believe the buzzard, which weighed about two pounds and had a thirty-inch wingspan, was probably protecting a nest.

"Buzzards are beautiful birds and are very common in Devon," said Emma Parkin of the RSPB. "They are normally very timid, but this one appears to have lost its fear of man and clearly must have a nest close by which it is protecting."

For whatever reason, the buzzard targeted cyclists but ignored runners who were training in the same area for an upcoming half marathon.

Parkin said painting large eye shapes on cycling helmets would help repel the bird. Several cyclists followed her suggestion, and the buzzard left them alone. But it still had unresolved anger management issues.

It finally met its demise when it foolishly tried to attack a van. The RSPB said the aggressive bird of prey was accidentally killed after it zoomed down and struck the vehicle near Holsworthy.

Parkin, who said it was unusual for buzzards to attack humans, thought it was likely the buzzard was one of a pair and that the surviving bird would now care for the chicks. "There is probably a single parent buzzard flying around now," she said at the time. "I hope that's the case. The chicks should be pretty robust by now anyway, but this will definitely mean their chances of survival have diminished."

As for the angry buzzard, she said, "it was just being a good parent, although it was probably rather too enthusiastic."

A wild goose that misjudged its landing slammed into a teenage skateboarder.

The low-flying Canada goose was heading for a pond in Winnipeg in 2002 when it apparently flew off course and smacked into the face of thirteen-year-old Shawn Hacking, knocking him off his skateboard. The teen suffered two badly scraped knees, a sprained wrist, a ripped shirt, and a red face where the bird's wing slapped him.

Shawn's friend Brent Bruchanski told the *Winnipeg Free Press*, "It was so funny, but I felt sorry for him at the same time. It flew out of nowhere and then . . . wham bam!"

Shawn's mother Kim Hacking said, "When he came in, he said, 'I got hit by a goose.' I thought that was some kind of car or something."

When authorities in northeast Scotland tried to scare off swarms of seagulls by using robotic birds of prey, the gulls fought back—and won.

Because they are noisy, messy, and annoying, the area's 2,000 seagulls have been a constant problem in the coastal towns of Scotland.

Fowl-Ups

In declaring war on the gulls, the Aberdeenshire Council turned to modern technology for help. For a three-week trial period in 2003, environmental officers strategically placed five robotic peregrine falcons on rooftops around the seaside town of Fraserburgh. Each robot—or Robop (which stands for Robot Bird of Prey)—was programmed to perform a menacing repertoire of wing flaps, head turns, and calls. Authorities hoped the seagulls would be so frightened by the fake birds that they would fly off, reducing the number of nesting birds in the town.

But the gulls were far from being scared. Within a week, the gulls were doing their best to intimidate the Robops, admitted environmental health manager Colin Campbell. "In some cases, the seagulls have been ganging up on the [fake] birds and trying to scare them off," he told the Scottish newspaper the *Herald*. "It seems that the main problem was the sheer volume of gulls that the Robops faced."

When the three-week trial had ended, Campbell conceded it was "a victory for the stubborn sea birds."

Winged Wonders

Smart-Thinking Birds

BARN SWALLOWS MIGHT BE SMARTER than you think.

Several of the birds apparently have figured out how to operate the motion-detector doors at a Home Depot store in Maplewood, Minnesota, so they can go in and out while raising their brood in their indoor nests—safe from weather and predators.

"I thought this is so unusual that it needs to be recorded and put in the book of knowledge on barn swallows," Keith Stomberg, a Home Depot store supervisor, told the St. Paul *Pioneer Press* in 2004. "This takes deductive reasoning. The term 'birdbrain' now has got to be modified."

Stomberg said he first noticed the birds nesting inside the store in the summer of 2001. He was fascinated by their apparent learned behavior and left them alone to raise their families. What really amazed him was that at least one pair learned that if they flew in a tight circle in front of the motion detector above the double doors at the entry to the store, the doors opened. Each bird then zoomed inside where the pair had built a nest atop a small pipe near the ceiling. When a bird was ready to leave, it flew in a tight circle in front of the motion detector inside the doorway until the doors opened again.

"One of the assistant managers locked the door early,"

Stomberg recalled. "The barn swallows weren't done [going in and out] yet. They actually picked at him and harassed him until he unlocked the doors like, 'Hey! Unlock the doors, dummy! I'm not done feeding my kids!'"

In 2003, Stomberg contacted the staff of the Nongame Wildlife Program of the Minnesota Department of Natural Resources. The DNR officials who came to investigate were skeptical, he said, but when they saw the swallows open the doors by circling near the motion sensors, the officials "picked their jaws up off the floor."

"It's very interesting and amazing to watch that they can make this work to their advantage," Steve Kittelson, a DNR wildlife specialist, told the newspaper. "It certainly gives them a secure site for nesting. They've eliminated a lot of predators and weather elements. They even have air conditioning."

Carrol Henderson, nongame wildlife supervisor for the DNR, said the birds apparently remember the behavior from year to year and return to the same spot after winter migrations to Central and South America.

"It expands our appreciation for the fact that there are lots of different birds and animals who may have intelligence greater than we acknowledge, but normally they don't have a way of expressing it," Henderson said. "In this case, they're doing something above and beyond normal behavior. Here's a little piece of technology where they figured out the motion detector."

After observing the nesting swallows, wildlife biologist Joan Galli told *Birder's World* magazine that she was amazed to see how the birds had adapted to the unique setting in order to raise their families. "We typically think of the crow family and the parrot family as among the most intelligent of birds," Galli said. "But apparently the swallows have a few tricks of their own that help us appreciate how birds are constantly adapting to survive in novel human-created environments."

By the summer of 2004, there were at least a dozen nests inside various entrances, said store manager Gregg Barker. "They'll operate all the doors," Barker told the *Pioneer Press*. "All of them do. To get inside, they'll flutter right underneath these sensors until it opens."

The store has become an attraction for bird-watchers. "One lady stops in once a week just to check them out," Barker said. "I had a couple of bird-watching groups who came and set up videos to tape them."

A smart cockatiel who lives in a tailor shop has customers in stitches—literally. That's because the brainy bird has learned to sew. He can pick up a pin and thread it through the material with his beak.

The nine-year-old bird, which goes by the name of Baggio, learned how to stitch after years of watching his owner, master tailor Jack Territo, work in his shop in Bristol, England.

"I've never heard of a bird that can stitch, but Baggio has a great sewing action," Territo, sixty, told reporters in 2004. "He has become a real hit with our customers."

Baggio's picture has appeared in dozens of publications throughout the world and he has even appeared on a British talent show for pets. Territo said his cockatiel impresses everyone with his needlework skills. "When people see what he can do, they're amazed. Other animals can do tricks but this bird can sew. There is no competition."

When it was covered in an oily goo and unable to fly, a seagull knew exactly where to go for help—the emergency room.

In 1976, while its brethren were sleeping shortly before dawn, the wild bird waddled into the ER of Utah Valley Hospital in Provo, Utah. Surprised staff members gave the bird a bath and some food and registered their new patient as J. L. Gull, in honor of the best-selling book *Jonathan Livingston Seagull*.

"We saw the bird just waddling down the hallway all dark and greasy," nurse Cheryl Giles told UPI. "Our door is usually open, and it just walked right in."

After being treated, J. L. posed for television cameras and

photographers. Veterinarians visited J. L. and determined it was sufficiently cleaned so that the bird could be put on the outpatient list. Later that evening, the Utah Fish and Game Department released the seagull at Utah Lake just west of Provo.

The bird's condition set off an investigation of possible oil spills in the area. Utah Lake was found to be clean, but officials discovered an oily scum at a nearby industrial holding pond, where many seagulls congregated.

Seagulls have been highly respected in Utah since 1847 when flocks of the birds saved the pioneer Mormons' crops by eating swarms of crickets that had blackened the sky. The citizens of Utah were so appreciative of the winged rescuers that they built a gold monument to the seagull and named it the state bird.

A tiny bird surprised naturalists by making an intrepid journey back to its former home just to be with its mate.

The male tomtit—a close relative of the common titmouse but with cobalt blue wings and tail—flew nearly 100 miles over water and unfamiliar territory so it could be by the side of its true love.

"This has shown he was able to make it back, dodging predators all the way and somehow getting enough food to get him there," New Zealand's Department of Conservation spokeswoman Rosalie Stamp told the *New Zealand Herald*.

The bird, named RG after a conservation department staff member, was one of thirty-two banded tomtits transferred in the spring of 2004 to an island wildlife sanctuary where a number of endangered species live. Weighing about a third of an ounce, tomtits are not endangered but are fully protected, fiercely territorial, and usually keep the same partner.

While the conservationists were catching tomtits, including RG, southeast of Auckland before the transfer, RG's mate eluded capture. The trapped tomtits were banded, put in a dark box, and taken by helicopter to the island sanctuary in the Hauraki Gulf. The birds had been moved to the island because it is pest-free.

But although it might have seemed heavenly for the other birds, it apparently was hell for RG without its mate. So even though the tomtit had no visual clues of how it arrived on the island, the bird relied solely on its own innate navigation system to head home. Braving the open sea and an unfamiliar landscape, RG rejoined its mate.

It's not known how long the journey took. The bird simply showed up at a monitoring and feeding site in the Hunua Ranges where it had been living before its capture three months earlier. Conservationists were stunned when they spotted the "RG" band on its leg. In the tomtit relocation program, RG is the only bird known to have snubbed its new home.

Unlike the much safer and idyllic island sanctuary, the Hunua Ranges are home to many predators including rats, weasels, and ferrets. But RG had earned the right to stay put, said project coordinator Barbara Hughes. She told the newspaper, "He's obviously a South Auckland bird with attitude who likes it tough."

Some homing pigeons love their home so much that nothing will stand in their way of returning—not even after their owner gave them away.

British champion breeder Dino Reardon, sixty-six, parted with his birds in 1997 after retiring from the pigeon-fancying business. He gave one of his best birds, Diana, to a Spanish breeder. But, incredibly, the first chance Diana had to fly off, she left Spain and headed straight to her former loft in London, 1,500 miles away.

Although Reardon was touched, he didn't want to take care of any birds, so he gave the pigeon to a fancier in Filey, seventy-five miles away. "Diana wouldn't settle so I visited her every day, and she perked up," Reardon told the *Times* of London. But when Reardon stopped visiting the bird after five months, Diana came looking for him and returned to her old perch. In desperation Reardon gave the bird to another pigeon fancier in nearby Skipton, in 1998 but after just two nights, she was back again. "It was unbelievable," he recalled. "She had smashed her way out of her roost and flown home."

Reardon finally gave up and allowed the pigeon to stay. Reardon told the *Times*, "She keeps coming home because she loves me and she loves her loft. But I don't have the loft any more, so she's living in a cardboard box." In honor of the bird's tenacity, he renamed her Boomerang.

But that wasn't the only bird who insisted on returning to Reardon. In 2001, Boomerang's brother Figo showed up near the home of his breeder five years after he had been given away as a baby.

The bird was found lying upside down in a field, nearly dead from exhaustion and with two broken legs. The person who found the pigeon contacted Reardon through the ring number, which Figo was still wearing on his leg.

Reardon didn't know how far Figo had flown, but he

believed the pigeon had traveled many miles to return to its original home. "The person I gave the bird to did not register him, so I don't know exactly where he has come from. He had flown a long way and was utterly exhausted," Reardon told the news organization Ananova in 2002.

"I have kept pigeons all my life and had them fly hundreds of miles. I've never seen a pigeon in such a condition. He's been so ill."

Reardon rigged a special harness so Figo could be suspended from the floor to keep the weight off his legs. For the first few days after Figo came home, Reardon carried the bird in the back of his car to check his condition.

After tenderly nursing the pigeon back to full health, Reardon said, "I guess some birds just love me too much."

If ever there was a homing pigeon determined to return to his owner, it was Bluey.

The champion bird was kidnapped and held by his captors for two months. Yet even though his wings had been clipped, Bluey managed to escape and then walked an untold number of miles trying to get back home.

"It's a remarkable tale; it's unbelievable, really," said British champion breeder Dino Reardon.

The champion racer was originally owned by fancier Billy Blackburn who lived in Nelson, Lancashire, England. "Bluey was really well known in the town. He bred two champions that were called the Bluey Brothers by the Nelson Pigeon Club," Reardon said.

When Blackburn died in 1991, Bluey was put under Reardon's care. He was using Bluey for breeding when the pigeon was stolen in 1995. He figured the kidnappers had taken Bluey so the bird could father a flock of potential champions that could be worth about $500 apiece.

No one expected to see Bluey again, but they hadn't counted on his courage and tenacity. Two months after the kidnapping, Bluey was spotted walking on the side of the road right next to his original loft at the former home of his first owner, Billy Blackburn.

Bird fancier Frank Nicholson, who had heard of the feathered celebrity's flying exploits, discovered the brave but exhausted pigeon tottering on the shoulder of the road. "I just walked up to him and picked him up," Nicholson told the local newspaper *This Is Lancashire*. "Usually they won't let you near them, but he never bothered. I'd heard of Bluey, but I didn't realize it was him. He had an address tag, so I called up Mr. Reardon. He couldn't believe it."

Reardon, who lived fifteen miles away from Bluey's first home, said the trauma of being kidnapped and then having to walk a great distance probably made the bird head for the home he had lived in the longest. It was also possible that the kidnappers lived closer to the bird's original loft than to Reardon.

"He'd had his wings cut, so I assumed there was no way he could have come back home," said Reardon. "I'm amazed he survived at all."

Homing pigeons usually find their way back home—even if it takes five years. That's what happened to at least two different birds.

In 1997, during a Royal Pigeon Racing Association race from Nantes, France, to their home in Manchester, England, all of owner Tom Roden's birds returned except a racing pigeon named Whitetail. He finally showed up a little late—in 2002.

Whitetail arrived back into his loft as Roden was taking his dog for a walk. Roden told the *Manchester Evening News* that Whitetail was in good condition. "I recognized him straightaway because of his white tail feathers, and his ring-number confirmed I was right," he said. "I was absolutely amazed. He must have a phenomenal memory to recognize his way home after all this time."

Roden figured that someone had been looking after Whitetail during those missing years. "I always said that I thought Whitetail would one day make his way back. He had won thirteen races in his lifetime and flown over the Channel fifteen times. But even I had begun to give up hope of seeing him again."

That's how pigeon fancier Oswald Drescher, of Germany, felt when his own homing pigeon failed to return from a 132-

mile flight from Wiesbaden in 1997. Normally, a homing pigeon can cover that distance in less than ninety minutes.

It took Drescher's bird five years. "I'd assumed she was gone and done for," Drescher told reporters in 2002. "Then she showed up the other day and went to a feed trough just as calm as you please, as though she'd never been away."

Drescher figured the bird became sidetracked and was given refuge by another fancier. But this pigeon clearly never forgot her intended destination. "It's amazing when you think about it," the breeder said. "After five years I'm not sure I could find my way back to an old address. But this bird certainly could—and did."

A woodpecker with a love for peanut butter was determined to get as much of it as he could.

As a licensed wildlife rehabilitator in Prescott, Arizona, Johni Duncan was given a young acorn woodpecker to raise in 2002. During that time, the bird, nicknamed Woody, became fond of peanut butter. Even after its rehabilitation and release into the wild, the bird would return to Duncan's back door or window looking for a treat.

"One day a friend parked his car in my driveway and Woody stopped by," Duncan recalled in *Birds & Blooms* magazine. "I gave him some of his favorite snack and he flew to a nearby pine tree. On the way to his perch, the bird accidentally dropped some of the peanut butter into the windshield wiper well of my friend's car."

The friend, who didn't bother cleaning it up, came back three days later. "When my friend returned for another visit, Woody must have remembered where he lost the treat," said Duncan. "The bird flew down to the car and immediately retrieved his leftovers.

"Even though many other cars had parked in the driveway since the incident, Woody knew which automobile held his stash. I thought it was simply amazing, but my son joked that Woody must have recognized the license number."

A house sparrow in Connecticut proved that its species can be pretty smart—and devious.

Also known as the English sparrow because it was introduced to the United States from England in the mid-nineteenth century, the bird is an aggressive species that will kill adult birds, nestlings, and eggs of other species in order to take over a birdhouse or nest.

The sparrow is also quite cunning, as evidenced by an 1877 report from an amazed bird-watcher in the *Hartford (CT) Times*. The birder had erected a large box for sparrows' nests in his backyard. It was divided into three rows, each containing four compartments. A dozen pairs of sparrows quickly claimed possession and went about making their nests.

"Sitting idly at the window one Sunday, watching the birds, the gentleman saw one cock sparrow come flying to his place with a fine, soft white feather in his bill," the article said. "He saw this bird fix the feather into an incomplete nest and then fly away.

"No sooner was [the male] out of sight than a female sparrow from the adjoining compartment, who had evidently seen [what the male did], hopped into her neighbor's house and pulled out and carried off the coveted feather. Becoming interested, the [human] observer watched the performance, expecting to see the little thief carry her stolen prize to her own nest; but no, she knew a trick . . . and here is where she displayed an undeniable reasoning process, and acted on a clear perception of cause and effect. . . . She flew off with the feather to a neighboring tree, where she secretly fastened it in an inconspicuous place upon and between two twigs and there left it.

"Pretty soon the bird she had defrauded came back with a straw to add to his nest. Discovering his loss, he came out with an angry chirruping that boded no good to the despoiler of his hearth and home, if he could only find the rogue. His first demonstration was to visit his next-door neighbor without any search warrant. In that abode of peace and innocence he found no trace of the stolen feather, and as for the actual guilty party, she was hopping innocently about, and loudly demanding—as far as the bird tones could be understood by the man at the window—what was meant by this ungentlemanly intrusion.

"The cock sparrow was evidently puzzled. Unable, after a minute search, to find the lost feather, he apparently gave up and flew away in search of another.

"The thief demurely waited till he had got well off, and then flew to the tree, secured the stolen feather, and took it in triumph to her own nest."

A farmyard goose has been clever enough to know that at Christmastime, it needs to flee to a safe haven so it doesn't end up as the main course for a holiday dinner.

Every December, the goose shows up at the Wildfowl and Wetlands Trust in Gloucestershire, England. The goose, believed to be from one of the farms near the sanctuary, settles in with rare swans at the nature reserve.

"We first noticed the intruder in 2001, though he blends in quite well with the throng of Bewick's swans we feed each day," Dave Paynter, manager of the sanctuary, told BBC News Online. "I was really surprised when I saw him again this winter, but he is certainly a devious chap.

"We have no idea which farm he comes from, but he is clever enough to know he needs to make a hasty getaway at this time of year to avoid being served up as someone else's dinner."

A cunning turkey called Cranberry must have taken a cue from the goose. The gobbler saved itself from ending up on the Christmas dinner table by staying on the farm roof. Rather than hang out with the other 250 free-range turkeys that roam around Beechenwood Farm in Culverstone, Kent, England, the clever Norfolk black preferred to keep out of the way. Farmer Brian Hill joked that because he has been "up to his feathers" in work, he has been unable to reach the naughty gobbler, so the bird was saved from slaughter.

"Cranberry isn't stupid like the other turkeys," Hill told BBC News Online shortly before Christmas 2004. "He has stayed on the farm roof since the summer because he wants a bird's-eye view of us working and of the other farm animals. It's really unusual because most turkeys stick together, even when a fox comes along.

"But Cranberry is far too clever for that. He knows Christmas is coming and he's going to be saved from the dinner table by staying on the roof."

Hill said that because Cranberry was such a character, the farmer will keep it for a few years. "I think he will have fun on the farm next year because there will be only one male turkey and sixteen hens."

A parrot wowed patrons of a Long Island restaurant for years by whistling operatic arias.

From the 1930s through the 1950s, Coco the African gray would sit on an old nickelodeon in the bar of Villa Victor, a French restaurant near Syosset, and whistle opera favorites. His musical talent was first noticed when he learned to whistle the C major scale while perched on a piano in the back room. The waiters had unintentionally taught him by running a finger over the keyboard as they passed between the kitchen and the dining room.

When Coco mastered the scale, the waiters taught him classic opera tunes. He was then moved from the back and into a cage in the main dining room. There he would delight the patrons by whistling songs from a repertoire that included "The Drinking Song" from *La Traviata*, the "Funeral March" from *Aida*, "Hall of the Mountain King" from *Peer Gynt*, and parts of arias from *La Bohème* and *Carmen*.

"Before each rendition, Coco gives a little self-important squeak to signify that he is the number-one whistler and that the others should be silent," reporter Kenneth Love wrote after meeting the parrot in 1952. "It is a fact, he is better than all the others."

The parrot made his presence known in other ways too. "When he sees a pretty girl come into the bar, he gives a long, deliberate wolf whistle," said Love. "He shouts with laughter if the girl's escort turns angrily on the bartender."

Coco took no guff from the restaurant cats. "On fine

mornings, Coco walks about on the lawn, picking at blades of grass and imitating the songbirds," Love said. "The cats on the place are afraid of him. When one approaches, he ruffles his feathers and emits a fighting tomcat yowl. He can also bark like a dog."

That was enough to keep the cats away and make patrons of the restaurant admire Coco that much more.

A pet parrot testified in a court case, swaying the judge to detain the bird's accused abductor.

In 1903, in Hoboken, New Jersey, police arrested Peter Cadena on a charge of stealing Sapho, a garrulous Brazilian parrot owned by actress Selma Claret. Police accused Cadena of stealing Claret's feathered friend from Hoboken pet-sitter Anna Wendt, who was looking after the bird. But Cadena claimed that he had bought the parrot in a Hudson Street saloon.

At the preliminary hearing presided over by Judge Stanton in Hoboken, the *New York Times* stated that Sapho entertained the court with his whistling from his gilded cage, which sat next to the judge's bench. When Mrs. Wendt entered the courtroom, Sapho squawked, flapped his wings, and uttered, "*Ein, zwei, drei, vier!*"

"You see, Judge, he knows me," said Mrs. Wendt, who had been teaching the parrot to count in German and to speak a few phrases in the language. Then, addressing the parrot directly in court, she said, "Yes, dear, they shan't steal you from your Selma."

"Robber! Robber!" Sapho shouted. Then, speaking in German, the parrot said, "*Wo bist du*, Selma?" (Where are you, Selma?)

Impressed, the judge then asked Sapho directly, "To whom do you belong?"

The bird quickly responded, "Selma!"

"There is no doubt in this case," the judge declared. "This bird has proved an excellent witness, and I shall hold the prisoner on $300 bail on a charge of grand larceny."

When they saw one of their fellow birds die in a cold-blooded murder at a park zoo, three owls took matters into their own claws. Before the killer could make a clean getaway, the owls attacked and killed him.

The carnage happened in 1936 at the outdoor Trailside Museum of the American Museum of Natural History at Bear Mountain Park, New York. Staff members at the museum, which housed a small zoo featuring indigenous birds and other animals, were in mourning after the tragedy.

That's because the victim was the zoo's most popular attraction, Joe the crow, who had been a friend to kids and adults for nine years there. Sometime during the night, Joe was killed by Napoleon, the resident weasel that had gnawed through the fine-mesh wire encircling the crow's cage.

But the slayer's dastardly deed was avenged. While fleeing from Joe's cage, Napoleon was killed by the zoo's three barn owls—Tom, Dick, and Harry.

Joe was discovered murdered shortly before 7 a.m. by Steward Fisher, an employee. As he approached Joe's cage, Fisher shouted, "Good morning, Joe," but failed to receive the usual responding cheerful caw. Then he saw the bird's body lying on the ground beneath his perch.

Grief-stricken, Fisher immediately called William Carr, the museum director who reconstructed the crime for reporters:

Winged Wonders

Sometime during the night, the weasel, whom we call Napoleon—and we now call him something a lot stronger—bit his way through [his own] mesh wire cage. He made a hole about the size of a twenty-five-cent piece and managed to escape.

Joe's cage is about twenty-five yards away, and the weasel must have gone there immediately and slipped through the wire. From the slashes on Joe's body, the weasel must have first grabbed him by the leg and dragged him off the perch. Once on the ground, the weasel finished him off by biting his throat.

After killing Joe, the weasel left the cage from the side and that's where he made his mistake, for he ran right into the owls' cage. The owls apparently jumped on him and there must have been a terrible battle. One of the owls received some pretty bad scratches, but the weasel was torn to pieces.

The staff buried Joe on the lawn in front of his cage, and

the employees erected a small marker that said, "Here lies Joe, the children's friend."

The crow had been extremely popular. For the first two years of Joe's life at the museum, the staff let him remain free to move around. But because he had a fondness for stealing car keys and other small objects, Joe was finally put in a spacious cage. Confining the crow didn't dampen his spirits. A longtime favorite of children, Joe would caw and hiss when his name was called and would allow anyone to pet and feed him.

"I hope people won't think we are oversentimental about Joe, but Joe was a wonderful bird and he surely will be missed," Carr said. "Why, people used to come for miles just to see Joe and to call him up to the front of his cage and scratch his head. He had made thousands of friends."

Winged Wonders

A pet parrot that had flown off for a little adventure was captured by a wildlife official who was able to find his owners after the bird told her that his name was Basil.

The bright green eclectus parrot had escaped from the home of Ann Bradley of Swindon, England, in 2002. Previously, the bird had never flown more than a few yards from his home. But for some reason, he took off. Bradley, concerned about her parrot being out overnight, reported him missing to police. "I'm sure I heard his squawk the next morning," she told BBC News Online. But there was no visible sign of Basil.

Later the next day, RSPCA officer Debbie Sheppard found a parrot sitting on a garden fence and managed to capture him. While squawking a few phrases, including "good boy" and "tickle, tickle," the four-year-old bird spoke his name.

"My husband couldn't believe it when he started to talk," Sheppard told the BBC. "Basil was coming out with all sorts of things. Once he started, he couldn't stop."

Sheppard contacted police who checked records for a missing parrot named Basil. After they found a match, they called Bradley. "When we got a call to say he'd been found, we were absolutely delighted," she recalled.

Basil had flown from his home just a few streets away and was soon reunited with his owners.

Bradley said Basil was an excellent mimic. "He's just like a tape recorder. He'll copy the telephone and say 'hello' before we've had a chance to pick it up. He tells my children to get ready for school." And the next time Basil gets lost, he can simply tell officials his name.

Notorious Pet Birds

IN ONE OF THE MOST BIZARRE CONTESTS IN ANIMAL HISTORY,
a champion racing pigeon shamed the avian world by twice
losing a race to a greyhound in England in 2001.

The bird, named Speckled Jim, was specially trained to
fly four feet above the ground for up to 100 yards, and was
known to reach speeds of 70 mph. The five-year-old thirteen-
ounce bird trained by Dave Sleight was a United Kingdom

show sprint titleholder and had been unbeaten in twenty-seven races against other birds.

But no one knew how the racing pigeon would do against a greyhound named Althea Storm, who had won twelve of twenty races against other dogs.

An eighty-meter racetrack was set up at Wimbledon Greyhound Stadium. Both animals had to start from a trap or starting cage. Sleight was allowed to hold the bird in the trap and release him when the door sprang open. At the finish line was a cage where the bird's mate, Mrs. Jim, was waiting. A mechanical rabbit was the prey for Althea Storm to chase.

In individual time trials in the days before the race, both contestants had been registering almost identical times. The contest, which was closed to the paying public, drew plenty of interest from fans and the media—and especially bookies, who made the dog a slight favorite over the pigeon.

What a Hoot

At the start of the race, Speckled Jim fluttered to the ground for a brief second before zipping down the straightaway, but it was too late to catch his canine rival, who roared to victory in 5.3 seconds—a full second faster than the pigeon.

At Sleight's insistence, Speckled Jim and Althea Storm met again a few weeks later, this time at Belle Vue Stadium in Manchester in front of a raucous crowd. Speckled Jim was hoping to settle an old score and make the dog spit feathers this time around, Sleight told reporters before the second race.

"Jim fluffed his lines at Wimbledon," admitted his trainer. "He missed the break from the traps and the dog had too much early pace for us, but I promise you it will be a different story this time around. Jim has been training well and he starts quicker now. He has been on a high protein diet. We slapped a no-sex ban on him two weeks ago, so our lad will be safe at home with Mrs. Jim before Althea Storm is halfway down the straight."

Althea Storm was a strong favorite to repeat his success over the seventy-five-yard course. "Bring it on!" shouted the dog's trainer, Brett Capaldi, moments before the race. "[Jim] flaps and he flies when he hears the gun, but he can't take his eyes off my dog's bum! 'The Storm' has done nothing but improve since Wimbledon, and if anything, we will beat Jim easier this time around. This dog is like a fine wine, full-bodied and improving with age. The only way that overhyped piece of poultry is going to beat us at Belle Vue is if he hitches a lift on the [mechanical] hare!"

The bookies agreed with Capaldi's assessment, making the greyhound a solid favorite, although most everyone figured the race would be a lot closer this time. In solo trials at Belle Vue Stadium, a strong tailwind helped Speckled Jim nearly double his speed, David Hood, spokesman for the sponsors of the race said.

But when it counted most, the bird failed again, getting outpaced by the greyhound in their rematch. Althea Storm led from the start and won by four lengths. The dog got a great jump and stayed in the lead all the way. "Unfortunately, we got such a big crowd here that the pigeon seemed a bit put off, and kept veering to the left," John Gilburn, general manager of Belle Vue said.

"There would have been a lot of humiliation if 'The Storm' had been beaten by a corn-fed piece of poultry," Capaldi said.

A beer-swigging pet parrot that thought of himself as one of the regulars at a local pub was temporarily banned for unruly behavior.

Lee Jones, landlord of the Penrhys Inn in Rhondda, south Wales, announced in 2001 that he was barring the parrot, named Captain, from public areas because his antics had become so bad. Jones told reporters that the bird was copying the behavior of regulars—drinking from pints, taking cigarettes from packs on the bar, and even swearing. And whenever a female customer walked into the pub, Captain greeted her with a loud wolf whistle.

"He has picked up some swear words and uses them to heckle the men playing pool," Jones said at the time. "But the worst thing is his wolf whistling. Women hear a loud whistle when they walk in and they think it's me."

Jones said he ran out of patience with Captain's behavior. "We bought Captain as a novelty but he is a right rascal and we can't trust him anymore," Jones told the BBC. "To start with, it was good fun to see him swoop onto a customer's shoulder to get a free drink. But he's got a taste for beer now and he's always got a cigarette in his mouth although he's not learned to light them yet."

The bird was banned only for a few days before the pub's regulars demanded the return of Captain. Jones gave in and the parrot once again drank and swore with the customers.

Jones's daughter Samantha, seventeen, said, "Captain is a typical bloke. You can tell when he's been drinking because he doesn't get up until midday."

A magpie named Thatcher that had become a regular customer at a local pub was banned for life after he started filching food and beer from the patrons.

The troublemaking bird first started pecking on the windows of the King's Arms in Wakefield, England, in 2004 and fast became a favorite with the customers. But he soon began to wear out his welcome. "He got more and more used to people and started nicking [stealing] beer out of pint glasses," pub owner Alan Tate told BBC News Online. "His favorite is the Classic Blonde which we have [on tap]—he went mad for that. He used to squawk at people who used to hide their pints from him."

But Thatcher soon grew bolder and started swiping fries and then purloining food from patron's meals. "He had started walking on people's plates while they were eating and we had to refund a few meals," Tate said.

The bird's antics were no longer amusing. Tate banned Thatcher from the pub. Whenever the magpie tried to saunter into the building, he was firmly discouraged by the employees, who were concerned about health and safety rules. "I couldn't have him in the pub if I wanted to, so I had to bar him," Tate said. "If he comes in, I've found the best way to get him out is to use something shiny. I'd use my keys, he would come over and sit on them, and then I could carry him out."

Some patrons still wanted Thatcher, so Tate compromised and confined the magpie to the beer garden. But the bird continued to cause havoc and hilarity in roughly equal measure until Tate finally had to bar him from there as well. "It was getting too much," he said. "He was too mischievous and he used to attack children. He used to land on them and peck at their heads, which was funny to watch so long as it wasn't your kid."

Tate resisted suggestions by some to call in a pest control firm or have the bird shot. "He had to go, but I didn't want to do what some people suggested I do to him. He's amused us all. He's a character and I couldn't do that to him."

Instead, Tate resorted to locking Thatcher in the linen cupboard whenever he got too troublesome. But Tate admitted there was usually a treat of table scraps awaiting the bird when he was released at closing time.

An Amazonian green parrot that was about to make his stage debut was given the pink slip after turning the air blue during the final dress rehearsal.

Percy the parrot had landed the avian role in a production of *Pirates on Treasure Island* at the Jakes Ladder Theatre Company in Blandford, Dorset, England, in 1999. During early rehearsals Percy handled his one line perfectly, saying "Pieces of eight" right on cue every time.

But in the last rehearsal before opening night, the parrot didn't utter the line. Instead, he squawked a string of obscenities during rehearsals. First, the parrot said, "Piss off, mate." Assuming it was an innocent slip from an inexperienced thespian, the cast pressed on, but Percy then started chanting, "Bugger off, bugger off," followed by a series of even ruder words.

The cast was amused, but the director and producer decided they could not risk the foul-beaked parrot offending young members of the audience. Percy's owner was reportedly shocked by his behavior. The show went on, but without a live parrot.

It's one thing to be a potty-mouthed parrot. But it's another to be a potty-mouthed parrot that lives in a church.

In 2002, Charlie, a three-year-old African gray owned by Zarina France, thirty-four, of Yorkshire, England, escaped from his home. He didn't go very far, but no amount of cajoling or bribery could entice him to return to captivity. The mischievous parrot began living with a flock of pigeons in the bell tower at St. Mary's Church in nearby Mirfield.

And that's when Charlie started ruffling a few feathers of the churchgoers because he liked to let loose with several epithets and wolf whistles at passers-by. The vicar received complaints from people who became targets for verbal abuse from the exotic bird.

"Charlie can be very abusive and say all sorts of filthy things that I don't want to repeat," France admitted to reporters at the time. "He probably picked it all up from me, and when I heard about a swearing parrot I knew it was our

Charlie." France made several attempts to catch the parrot, but Charlie remained free as a bird for several months.

Church warden Stuart Wooller said Charlie had become a local celebrity since escaping from his owner during the summer. "I have spoken to Charlie several times and he seems quite happy at the church. I know that he wolf whistles but I haven't heard him swear at me, probably out of respect because I am the warden."

Yorkshire resident Tim Wood said he was shocked after hearing a mysterious voice from above as he walked his dogs in the churchyard. "I couldn't believe it when I first heard the parrot," he said. "I thought I must have really upset someone because of the language that was being used."

A mischievous performing hawk was forced to step down from its perch after it was involved in a series of embarrassing incidents with spectators.

For years, Harry the hawk had performed to appreciative crowds at the Thorp Perrow Arboretum near Bedale, North Yorkshire, England. But then in 2000 Harry began getting carried away.

In a routine known as a "dummy bunny," owner Tom Graham would throw a piece of brown fur into the audience for Harry, a Harris's hawk, to retrieve. On this particular day, the bird alighted on the head of a man in the audience. "Harry decided to use him as a perch," Graham recalled, "but unfortunately when he took off, he had the man's toupee in his feet. After flying off with the spectator's toupee, Harry tried to eat it, thinking it was live prey."

Another time, Harry punctured a large inflated castle where little children were bouncing around. Harry later

ruined part of an ice cream vendor's stock when the hawk
flew into the man's truck and landed in one of the tubs of
ice cream.

Despite the incidents, Harry continued to perform, but
in 2003 Graham decided it was time for the hawk to retire.
Now out of the limelight, the bird began breeding offspring.

"He just became too mischievous and was doing his own
thing," Graham explained to reporters. "He was losing his
fear of people. But he has been a brilliant bird over the
years. He is certainly a character."

A hand-reared raven with British royal connections
stunned its owner when, without any training, it began to
speak, telling him to "shut up" and ordering his dogs around.

Zeus the raven, whose father was one of the queen's famous flock of ravens at the Tower of London, unexpectedly started speaking when he was six months old. A year later, the bird, which was being groomed to be the star in a bird of prey exhibition, soon became a thorn in the side of owner Richard Cooper. That's because the raven began mimicking family and friends, much to Cooper's chagrin.

As well as telling its owner and others to shut up, Zeus orders Cooper's two pet dogs to sit and lie down. Zeus also laughs like Cooper's wife and taunts visitors to their home in Cumbria, England.

"My poor dogs don't know whether they are coming or going because he mimics my voice so perfectly," Cooper told reporters in 2002. "It is quite spooky sometimes. We have had people knock at the front door and they've heard a voice shout 'come in,' and they looked behind them to see who it was. Of course, there was nobody there." Just Zeus.

By 2004, Cooper had high hopes that Zeus, who has a wingspan of more than four feet, will become the star attraction at a traditional county show in Cumbria. "Zeus is a real crowd-puller," said a spokesman for the Cumbria Tourist Board. "We're hoping to teach him to say, 'Come back soon.'"

A lost cockatiel was driving his foster keeper to distraction by whistling Tchaikovsky's 1812 Overture every day for weeks—and always at the ungodly hour of four in the morning.

The gray and yellow bird had been rescued from a tree in Sunderland, England, in 2003 by members of the RSPCA and put in the foster care of Elaine Redhead, a volunteer who took in lost or abandoned pet birds. She named the cockatiel

Spikey, but she thought of several not-so-nice names for the bird after he showed off his early-morning musical specialty.

Redhead, who owned two parakeets and was also looking after a lost budgerigar, said that the newcomer's tuneful talent came as a shock. "The first time it happened I was out in the garden and when I came in my husband said the bird had been whistling the tune," Redhead told reporters. "He repeated it and I recognized straightaway that it was the 1812 Overture. Spikey's rendition of Tchaikovsky's piece is pretty impressive."

It was cute the first time—but it got old real quick. Just before dawn for three weeks straight, Spikey shattered the peace of Redhead's home. "Every morning at 4 a.m., he stands to attention and starts whistling, which sets all the other birds off and wakes everyone up," Redhead said at the time.

She and her husband James went to the London press and pleaded for the cockatiel's owner to come forward.

"Someone must have taken a lot of time and trouble in training him, so I'm sure they are missing him and it's only right that he should go back to his true owner," she said. "When that happens, we'll be sorry to see him go but very relieved to get a proper night's sleep."

Finally, after three weeks, the cockatiel's owner contacted the RSPCA. The owner, Etta Clinton, from Sunderland, said she had been on vacation and wasn't aware that her bird—whose real name was Zak—had been found. She said Zak had escaped when he opened the unlocked door to his cage, which was out in her garden. Clinton added that Zak had been taught the 1812 Overture by his previous owner.

Redhead was thrilled to return Zak to his rightful owner. "Now I'll be able to get some sleep," she said.

When neighbors heard yelling and screaming, police were called to deal with what everyone assumed was a domestic dispute. It was, except the family feud wasn't between a man and a woman, but between two angry parrots.

It happened in 2003 in Remscheid, Germany, near Dusseldorf. Occupants in an apartment building became concerned when they heard loud screams coming from one of the apartments. Fearing that the verbal battle could escalate into a bloody brawl, one of the neighbors phoned police.

According to the police report, the woman living in the flat "kindly opened the door and unmasked the two culprits." They turned out to be her two parrots, who appeared to be involved in a screaming match. "They were arguing so loudly it really sounded like human screams," the statement said.

What a Hoot

A female vulture has become a regular visitor to a German beer garden. But rather than pay for her food like other patrons, she snatches lunches from customers.

The griffin vulture named Mary lives at a nearby falconry center in Riedenburg, Bavaria. She has been returning to the bar ever since 2002 when drinkers fed her after she crash-landed there.

Mary's owner, Margit Hafner, told the newspaper *Sueddeutsche Zeitung* that the fifteen-pound bird, which has a wingspan of almost nine feet, crashed during a bad thermal breeze. "Some guests fed her meat, so now she keeps wanting to return."

Josef Fuchs, the owner of the beer garden, said the vulture visits regularly and in her first summer there she had stolen ten pork chops. "Of course, my guests get a new helping if the vulture sits on their plates," he said.

Bobby the parrot had such a taste for booze that he became an alcoholic and had to be weaned off the hard stuff.

"The first time we let Bobby out of his cage he flew straight over to a pint of beer that my husband was drinking," owner Maria Radoi, of Bucharest, told the Romanian newspaper *Libertatea* in 2002. "He took a real liking to it. After that, he moved on to the harder stuff—whiskey and brandy. After that, we couldn't stop him."

Radoi said she initially thought it was doing Bobby no harm because he became more talkative after a drink. "He would say really nice things like, 'Kiss me, mum.' But then he became very demanding and chanted, 'beer, beer, beer' over and over again. It became an addiction."

So every day they gave Bobby a little less booze until he got used to life without alcohol. To ease the craving for the hard stuff, the couple got their parrot a mate to keep it company—but not as a drinking buddy.

A foul-mouthed parrot that's been the mascot on a British warship for several years caused crewmembers to hold their collective breath when the queen paid a visit in 2004.

The parrot, an African gray named Sunny, had embarrassed the crew several times before with her salty language after VIPs and even sailors' family members had come onboard the frigate HMS *Lancaster*.

As the ship's mascot since 2000, the bird has learned to swear like a drunken sailor. In addition to the earthier words and phrases like "*Annus horribilis*," she likes to squawk such phrases as "You ain't seen me, right?" and "Zulus, thousands of 'em!" from the 1964 film *Zulu*. She also learned to whistle the theme song from the 1963 film *The Great Escape*.

"She learns new words all the time and mimics what people say," logistics officer Lt. Commander John Pheasant told reporters shortly before the queen's visit.

The bird often pecks at people whenever she's in a bad mood. "I was a bit frightened of her at first," admitted Pheasant. "But she only pecks when she's really annoyed."

Sunny is the *Lancaster*'s second parrot. In 2000 while the ship was docked at its base in Portsmouth, the parrot's predecessor, Jenny, escaped from the bridge, was caught by a gust of wind, and blown into the water. An officer dived into the Portsmouth harbor in an attempt to save her, but couldn't reach her in time.

Sunny, who has the official service number RN Parrot Number 1, has lived in a large cage in the wardroom. And, as parrots do, she has taken to memorizing certain key words and expressions and then repeating them at unexpected and occasionally inopportune moments. Prominent among her repertoire is a range of anatomical expletives.

Sunny's most memorable outburst came during a visit by top navy brass in 2001. Despite being hidden in a broom closet, the parrot could clearly be heard as she let loose a string of four-letter words. Sunny's volley of verbal abuse was overheard by the fleet's commander in chief, Admiral Alan West, but he ignored her and carried on briefing the crew.

So it was no wonder crewmembers were quite concerned as they prepared for the arrival of the queen and Prince Philip.

Given Sunny's embarrassing track record in greeting high-level official visitors, the British press reported that the parrot would be given a forced shore leave during the royal tour. But the ship's captain, Commander Paul Chivers, wanted all crewmen on board, and that included Sunny, because she was part of the crew. Rather than being kept safely out of the queen's earshot in Portsmouth Naval Base for the duration of the visit, Sunny was left in her wardroom, which just so happened to be designated as the queen's private retiring room.

So what happened when the parrot met the royal couple? Sunny did not let the crew down. The bird kept a civil tongue.

What a Hoot

A captive parrot that had heard a couple making love repeated the sex talk the next day at a wildlife sanctuary.

According to the London newspaper *Sunday People*, Wendy Abel, thirty-nine, a warden at the Gentle Shaw Bird of Prey and Animal Centre, had taken a blue and gold macaw named Oliver home for the night in 2002. Later that evening, Wendy and her boyfriend Neil Tatler were acting like two eager lovebirds, all within earshot of the parrot.

Sunday People reported that after Abel returned to the sanctuary the next day, she was shocked and embarrassed when Oliver started squawking kisses and phrases like "God, oh, God," "Bouncy boo," and "How do you like it?"

Abel told the paper, "As soon as I heard what he was saying, I raced over to quiet him down. I knew exactly where he had picked up all that rude stuff—and so did everyone else."

Her boss Rob Smith said that Oliver's attention to detail left nothing to the imagination. "It sounded like he was reliving every moment from the night before," said Smith.

Abel's boyfriend said he wasn't embarrassed. In fact, he found the whole situation funny. "It was certainly a passionate night," Tatler told the newspaper. "When I heard what had happened I thought it was hilarious."

The macaw was kept away from visitors for several days while Abel tried to make him forget what he had heard coming from her bedroom.

A married Chinese man ran into some major mynah problems when the family bird reportedly spilled the beans on his marital indiscretions.

What a Hoot

According to a 2001 account in the newspaper *Xinmin Evening News*, the man's wife had returned from a month-long visit to her parents. She suspected something was wrong when their pet mynah bird began repeating words apparently picked up from her husband's secret telephone calls to his lover.

Words such as "divorce," "I love you," and "be patient" had become an increasingly frequent feature of the feathered tattletale's idle chattering. The bird became particularly talkative whenever the phone rang.

The woman, from the southwestern city of Chongqing, said she already suspected her husband was having an affair but the mynah's loose talk confirmed her suspicions.

According to the paper, the woman took her case— along with the bird—to a divorce attorney for consultation, hoping the mynah would be able to testify in court against her husband. The attorney wasn't optimistic that the bird's testimony would sway the court. "The judges are unlikely to rule against your husband based only on the mynah's words," the attorney reportedly told her.

In 2002, a cockatoo lived up to his gangster name by turning into a destructive hoodlum.

The bird, called Pretty Boy Floyd (named after an associate of mobster Al Capone), became a winged terror when his owner Mike Gepp was building a new guesthouse in Nelson, New Zealand. The cockatoo chewed up wiring at the guesthouse, wrecked the kitchen, and damaged a nearby car. Not only that but when he accompanied Gepp into town, the bird tore up leaflets in a bank and stopped traffic by walking in the road.

What a Hoot

Pretty Boy Floyd was such a terror that Gepp temporarily banished the bird to an animal sanctuary so he could finish building the guesthouse. "He had to go," Gepp told the local newspaper the *Nelson Mail*. "As fast as we were building, Floyd was pulling it all down."

The cockatoo was kept at Natureland in Tahunanui, where he had been hatched and reared before being adopted by Gepp. But like his gangster namesake, Pretty Boy Floyd tried his best to break out of his confinement. At the time, curator Gail Sutton said, "We keep having to change his cage, because he chews through things."

A pet parrot that had been left home alone and out of its cage was so bored it turned on a faucet to amuse itself.

The owner wasn't amused—especially after he returned home to a flooded apartment.

According to the Dutch newspaper *Utrechts Dagblad*, Jan Borst of Utrecht, the Netherlands, let his parrot out of its cage and then left it home alone for Christmas in 2001. Several hours later, neighbors in the apartment directly below his called the fire department after they saw water dripping from their ceiling.

When firemen arrived, they busted into Borst's apartment and discovered the tap that was connected to the washing machine had been turned on. The faucet was right next to the parrot's open cage. Borst said the bird sometimes played with the tap, but he never thought the bird could actually turn it on. The flood caused more than $5,000 damage.

What a Hoot

A parrot screaming like a damsel in distress sent police and firefighters rushing to the scene of the "crime."

In 2003, a police dispatcher in Tucson, Arizona, received a 911 hang-up call that apparently was made from the house. When police arrived, they found the house was locked with bars on the windows. Hearing what they thought was a woman's panicky, screaming voice, police called the fire department. Crews used a pry bar and a battering ram to bust down the door.

After police burst into the house, they soon realized that the screams weren't coming from a woman in trouble but from Oscar, a two-year-old yellow-naped Amazon parrot. Police found him intermittently making laughing and screaming sounds as he sat inside his large white cage. "The parrot's screams sounded identical to those of a distressed adult female," said Officer Andrew Davies.

Police asked a neighbor to call Dana Pannell, the home-owner who was at work at the time. Although the identity of the caller remained a mystery, the parrot was seemingly off the hook because Pannell's wife, Judy, said Oscar doesn't know how to use a phone. She told the Associated Press that Oscar was named after the *Sesame Street* character because of his foul moods.

Neighbors in the town of Wildemann, Germany, complained to the police that they were being disturbed day and night by the sound of a circular saw. What was so strange was that no one in the immediate area used such a power tool.

A police investigation in 2001 tracked the noise to a

house and identified the culprit—a parrot that perfectly mimicked the circular saw. The owner explained he had bought the bird cheap from a man who lived next door to a carpenter's workshop. The new owner claimed he tried everything to persuade the parrot to make a different noise, but without success. He was so fed up he gave the circular-saw-mimicking bird to an animal shelter.

A pet crow with a penchant for larceny made headlines in 1942 when it kept stealing coins from a newsstand.

Gypsy, an audacious two-year-old crow, targeted Morris' Stationery Store in Bergenfield, New Jersey. Day after day, coins were taken out of the open coin box of Morris Siwoff's newsstand outside his store. The proprietor couldn't figure out who the thief was until one day he noticed Gypsy with a dime in its beak.

Word spread around town of the thieving crow, and soon Gypsy became the subject of a feature story in the *New York Times*. The bird's owner, twelve-year-old Bobby Gillies, said a friend gave him the crow. Bobby taught the bird to come when it was called, but the boy made a point to say he never taught Gypsy to steal money.

Despite being the victim of an avian thief, Siwoff refused to press charges against the bird. "He's my friend," he told the *Times*. "I don't mind climbing up on things to get back the change" that Gypsy had stolen and hid.

"He's smart, that bird," Siwoff said. "You should see him walk up the street and make the cars go around him. Everybody around here knows him. He likes to play games with me. I wish he would take the pennies, though, and leave the silver."

Gypsy didn't target only the newsstand. The crow stole from home too. Bobby's mother, Mrs. Daisy Gillies, said that the beady-eyed vandal had made off with countless thimbles, buttons, rings, and trinkets. "He tries to hide things up on the roof where we can't find them," she told the paper.

During the interview in the Gillies' living room, Gypsy perched on the back of the reporter's chair. The bird then hopped down onto the arm of the chair and tried to remove the reporter's wedding ring, but the band was too tight so Gypsy gave up. Next, it flew to the front door and cawed twice—its way of asking to be let outside.

Unfortunately for Gypsy, one day of fame turned into a moment of shame.

The day after the feature story appeared in the *Times*, Gypsy was taken into custody by an agent for the ASPCA and charged with scratching a small child. According to authorities, the bird was winging its way to Siwoff's newsstand when it spotted two small children eating muffins on their unscreened front porch. Gypsy swooped down, pecked at a muffin, and then flew off, but during its brief visit, it left one of the children with a tiny scratch on his chest. The boy's mother called police. They summoned an ASPCA agent who nabbed Gypsy at the newsstand and took the crow away.

When Bobby found out what had happened, he called the ASPCA and pleaded his case, but to no avail. He was given three choices: destroy the bird, keep it permanently penned, or exile it from Bergenfield. He chose exile.

A few days later, Bobby took his pet bird to a friend twenty-five miles away and released it in the woods where there were no shiny coins, thimbles, ice cream cones, muffins, or newsstands. "He'll get along somehow," Bobby told a reporter. "He's smart. But I hope he doesn't think it [exile] is my idea."

Pet crows have been given a bad name—especially if that name is Blackie. The moniker is almost a guarantee that the bird will get into trouble.

For example, Blackie the pet crow loved to fly over the town of Verona, New Jersey, looking to steal cigarettes. The insolent bird would pilfer whole packs of smokes that were left outside on back porches.

In 1941 Verona police received a call claiming Blackie "snatched two packages of cigarettes from a backyard table and then, having opened them, tantalized his pursuers by perching on a chimney and dropping the cigarettes one by one."

Another pet crow named Blackie was persona non grata in the small town of Little Ferry, New Jersey, because of his antics. According to a contemporary news report in 1948, "Blackie refused to stop yanking clothespins off Monday washlines. And as weary women scooped sheets, shirts, and underwear from the ground, Blackie decorated the neighboring treetops with socks, handkerchiefs, and towels.

"Motorists were his victims on Saturday, holidays, and during summer vacation. When he tired of swooping in front of car windshields, he would strut slowly across a busy intersection and tie up traffic on several streets.

"Sunday may be a day of rest for some, but Blackie had other plans. He flew to the church belfry and cawed at the choir below."

The police chief, Charles Schedivy, felt compelled to take action and threatened to turn the crow into dinner unless owner William Slavik, fourteen, kept Blackie permanently out of trouble. William reluctantly put the crow in an escape-proof coop.

Another crow named Blackie made the news by getting drunk. When the pet of Mrs. Thomas Glass, of Cincinnati, took off one day in 1952 and failed to return, she contacted the media for help. She mentioned that "Blackie likes his beer."

Blackie apparently found someone who shared his love for beer and imbibed more than he should. A woman who heard about the missing bird found Blackie drunk as a loon, staggering up her driveway. Relieved that her pet was home—although he was suffering from a nasty hangover—Mrs. Glass said Blackie was probably enticed by "someone who heard about his taste for beer" and deliberately got him soused.

Then there was Blackie the crow who thought he was a seagull. When trying to land in the pool of his owner's cousin in Conklin, New York, in 1986, Blackie plunged under the water and began to drown.

Seeing the bird in distress, Pamela Hoover, thirty-nine,

dived into her pool and pulled Blackie out. Then, using a technique she recently learned while watching television, Hoover began mouth-to-beak resuscitation while pushing on his chest. Within a couple of minutes, Blackie was revived, apparently with no ill effects.

Wings of Valor

Heroic Birds

ONE OF THE HEROES IN WORLD WAR I was a valiant carrier pigeon named Cher Ami.

Despite being severely wounded, the bird flew through a salvo of enemy gunfire to deliver a message that helped save the lives of nearly 200 American soldiers.

During the war, the U.S. Army Signal Corps was given 600 carrier pigeons to ferry messages whenever signal flags or field phones failed or were unavailable. The pigeons, donated by bird breeders from Great Britain, were trained by American soldiers and used mostly in the Meuse-Argonne Offensive, a two-month battle in France that helped end the war.

Here's how the system worked: When a field commander needed to send a message, he wrote it out on paper and gave it to a Signal Corps soldier, who put it into a metal canister and attached the container onto the carrier pigeon's leg. After being tossed in the air, the bird flew back to its home coop in the rear. When it entered its coop, the pigeon tripped a wire that sounded a bell or buzzer, alerting a Signal Corps soldier that a message had arrived. He would run to the coop, remove the message from the canister, and then send it by telegraph, field phone, or personal messenger to the recipient.

For carrier pigeons, it was extremely hazardous duty.

Enemy soldiers knew that these birds were carrying important messages, and tried to shoot them out of the sky.

Cher Ami, French for "Dear Friend," was the most famous World War I carrier pigeon. The registered black check cock flew twelve missions along the front lines, but none more important than the message it carried on October 4, 1918.

Two days earlier, Major Charles Whittlesey had led more than 500 men from the 77th Infantry in an attack that broke through the enemy lines in the dense Argonne Forest. The major had his men set up defensive positions in a ravine. That night enemy soldiers surrounded the lone battalion, which was running low on food and ammunition. Then the Germans launched a full-scale assault on the battalion with machine guns, rifles, and grenades. Unfortunately, the American commanders didn't know the exact location of Major Whittlesey's men, and began firing hundreds of artillery shells into the ravine where the battalion was trapped. Hundreds died from American artillery and German firepower.

With his men being shelled by friendly fire, Major Whittlesey called for his last pigeon—Cher Ami. He wrote a quick note that said, "We are along the road parallel to 276.4. Our own artillery is dropping a barrage directly on us. For heaven's sake, stop it." The note was put in a canister on the bird's left leg.

As Cher Ami tried to fly back home, the Germans saw him rising out of the brush and opened fire. The bird was hit and fluttered toward the ground. It looked like the little pigeon wasn't going to make it. The American infantrymen were crushed; their only chance of ending the shelling seemed doomed to die.

But somehow the brave bird spread his wings and started climbing again, higher and higher, until he was beyond the range of the enemy guns. Cher Ami then flew twenty-five miles in only twenty-five minutes to deliver the message.

When he finally reached his coop, Cher Ami was badly wounded and lying on his back, covered in blood. He had been blinded in one eye, and shot in the leg and through his breast, making a hole the size of a quarter. His nearly severed leg was hanging by just a few tendons, and a silver canister with the all-important message was attached to that leg.

A short time later the shelling stopped. After five days the Lost Battalion was found and rescued. Of the 500 men, only 194 tired, hungry men marched wearily out of the forest. They survived because of the heroism of their leaders—and because of a little bird named Cher Ami who refused to give up.

Though the medics saved the bird's life, they couldn't save his leg, so a soldier carved a small wooden leg for him. When Cher Ami was well enough to be shipped from France to the United States, he was given a send-off by General John J. Pershing, commander of the United States Army.

Back in the United States, Cher Ami's touching, inspiring story filled columns in newspapers and magazines across the country. The bird became one of the most famous heroes of World War I. Sadly, he never fully recovered from his war wounds and died less than a year later. A taxidermist preserved the pigeon for future generations. Cher Ami is on display in Washington, D.C., at the Smithsonian Institution's National Museum of American History in the Armed Forces History Hall. Alongside the Croix de Guerre that was awarded to the bird by the French government, is the small silver capsule that held the all-important message that saved survivors of the Lost Battalion from being annihilated by friendly fire.

During World War II, 3,000 soldiers and 150 officers of the U.S. Army Pigeon Service were in charge of 54,000 military pigeons. The pigeons were used in every combat theater, and saw service with ground troops, on submarines, in bombers, and within the intelligence service. They flew in bad weather, at night, and through a hail of bullets—all while dodging birds of prey.

Arguably the most outstanding military pigeon in the war was G.I. Joe, who is credited with saving the lives of at least 1,000 British troops. Here's what happened, according to Otto Meyer, former commander of the U.S. Army Pigeon Service:

The British 56th Brigade had orders to attack the town of Colvi Vecchia, Italy, at 10 a.m., October 18,

1943. Just prior to their assault, the U.S. Air Support Command was scheduled to bomb the city to soften up the German defenses for the British brigade.

But rather than put up a fight, the Germans retreated, leaving only a small rear guard. As a result, the British troops entered Colvi Vecchia with little resistance and occupied it well ahead of schedule. All attempts made by radio and other standard means of communication to cancel the bombing of the town had failed. Time was running out.

So G.I. Joe—a seven-month-old dark checker pied white flight cock—was released carrying the important message to scrub the air assault. He flew twenty miles in twenty minutes back to the U.S. Air Support Command base, and arrived just as the American bombers were warming up to take off. If he had arrived a few minutes later, it might have been a tragic story.

General Mark Clark, commanding the U.S. Fifth Army, estimated that G.I. Joe saved the lives of at least 1,000 British allies.

In November 1946, the bird was shipped to London, England, where he was awarded the Dickin Medal for gallantry by the Lord Mayor of London. G.I. Joe was the first animal in the United States to receive Britain's highest animal award.

After the war the winged hero was placed with the Detroit Zoological Gardens where he died in 1961, at the age of eighteen. G.I. Joe was mounted and placed in the Historical Center, Meyer Hall, at Fort Monmouth, New Jersey.

A pet parrot named Rupert squawked loud enough to wake up its sleeping owner after the house caught fire. The owner escaped, but the heroic bird was left for dead.

In 1998 horse breeder Lynn Norley, fifty-three, was living with her twelve-year-old African gray parrot and two pet dogs in a rented 150-year-old farmhouse in Malvern, Pennsylvania. Sometime during the night, a faulty electrical box ignited a fire in the house, which did not have any battery-operated smoke detectors.

Fortunately, Norley had a live, feathered smoke detector. She was jarred awake when Rupert began screeching an alarm from his cage two rooms away from Norley's second-floor bedroom. "I opened my bedroom door and was hit with a wall of heat and thick smoke," Norley told reporters. She frantically gathered up her pets, but Rupert looked like he was dead, so she bundled him in her bathrobe and placed the parrot in a shower stall. Then she tossed her two dogs from a second-story bathroom window and leaped out behind them. Shrubbery below the window broke their fall.

Although firefighters from four towns battled the raging blaze, the historic farmhouse was destroyed. But out of heartache came unexpected joy.

At daybreak Norley returned to the gutted home with friends and neighbors, hoping to find Rupert's body so she could give the parrot a burial befitting a hero. While sifting through the smoking rubble, one of her friends shouted, "He's alive! He's alive! And the bastard bit me!"

Incredibly, against all odds, the amazing parrot had survived the blaze. Rupert was rushed to the All Creatures Animal Hospital in Washington Township, New Jersey, where the parrot was hospitalized for smoke inhalation and an often-fatal fungal infection. During the bird's month-long stay, veterinarian Michael Weiss discovered that Rupert was really a female. (Parrots have no external sex organs.)

Norley didn't care. She was just glad that her winged hero was on the road to recovery.

Rupert became a local celebrity. A few months after the fire, Philadelphia's Please Touch Museum for Children named the parrot a twentieth-century hero. Then Rupert began appearing at fire-safety lectures at area schools where the bird showed off its best trick—imitating a smoke detector siren.

"I thank God every day that I'm alive, and it's all because of Rupert's courage," Norley said. "I would have stayed asleep and not been here to tell this story if it wasn't for Rupert."

A pet cockatiel helped save the lives of his owners after waking them up when their house caught fire.

Niki La Roche, from Norrflaerke, Sweden, said that the house would probably have burned down if it had not been for Gilbert, a three-year-old cockatiel. In 2003, La Roche and her boyfriend Torbjoern Sjoelander were jarred out of their sleep in the early hours by the sound of Gilbert shrieking in the next room. The Australian cockatiel raised the alarm after a lit candle that the couple had inadvertently left on a shelf sparked a fire in the bird's room.

"We recognized Gilbert's panicky cry and rushed into the room, which was on fire," La Roche told reporters. Gilbert, his feathers covered in soot, was cowering in a corner, squawking madly.

The couple managed to put out the fire on their own, but La Roche said had they awakened a few seconds later, the room would have been engulfed in flames. "I don't want to think of what might have happened if it hadn't been for Gilbert," she said.

A pigeon that a man had nursed back to health repaid him by scaring off a suspected con artist.

In 2002, Ron Lingham, a fifty-two-year-old civil servant from Lancashire, England, found an injured pigeon in his garden. Upon inspecting it, Lingham discovered the bird had a broken wing, so he brought the pigeon into his house and named it Bobo after an owl in the 1963 film *Jason and the Argonauts*.

Man and pigeon became close friends, so when the bird's wing had healed, Bobo decided to stick around. Lingham was glad it did.

About five months later, Bobo showed it had the heart of a guard dog.

A woman carrying a tin box knocked on Lingham's door and asked him to donate some money for a charity. There was something about her that caused Lingham to become suspicious and he asked her to leave.

When she refused, Bobo zoomed into action. The bird flew downstairs from a perch on the landing and flapped around the woman's head. The startled woman fled as Lingham called police. Later that day, according to the London newspaper the *Sun*, a woman was arrested in connection with the incident.

"I don't know if it was a charity con or she was trying to divert my attention to thieve," Lingham told the paper. "She would not leave and started pushing past me. It was very alarming. Then came Bobo attacking her. She's my heroine. She did what a guard dog would do."

A chicken with a special affection for people was turned into a trained therapist.

Ruby, a Rhode Island Red that lived on a Seattle farm, was so good at helping bring comfort to senior citizens and traumatized children that she was given a lifetime achievement award by the ASPCA in 2000.

Her owner Maureen Fredrickson had bought Ruby at a feed store because she wanted to add to her flock of other hens. She had no idea that the hen had a special gift. But the very next day, Ruby gave Fredrickson a clue that she was no ordinary chicken. "She walked up to me and stood on my feet," Fredrickson recalled. "I reached down and picked her up, and suddenly she started rubbing her head on my chin, softly clucking all sorts of chicken words. Ruby followed me around, came when she was called, and was the most amazingly social chicken I had ever known."

Fredrickson, a member of the Delta Society, an organization that tries to improve the quality of life of humans through service and therapy animals, decided to train Ruby as a therapy bird. The hen learned to wear a leash and a harness, sit in a basket, and to signal when she had to relieve herself.

"She likes people," her owner said. "She likes being petted by people. Ruby has never pecked at anyone's glasses or jewelry, which is unusual because chickens generally peck at shiny things. She 'talks' softly and rubs her head against everyone I've ever handed her to. If she sits on someone's shoulder during a visit, she is very gentle about getting down when she's had enough."

Ruby, now retired, specialized in working with abused

children and senior citizens to overcome trauma. "It gave the child something neutral and nonthreatening to interact with," said Fredrickson. "She allowed them to take that first step and open up."

Ruby once worked with a six-year-old girl who refused to speak because of years of physical and emotional abuse. After encounters with the chicken, the girl broke her silence and spoke to her family unceasingly about the chicken.

The therapy bird was so good at what she did that she appeared on CNN's *Accent Health* and the *Sally Jesse Raphael Show*. Recalled Fredrickson, "When we appeared on [Raphael's] show with a live audience and cameras all around, Ruby not only was relaxed but also calmly laid an egg on the air. Unflappable!

"She was once with me in Chicago at a conference where there were more than fifty dogs. Never fazed her. She even reprimanded a golden retriever with a gentle nose peck when he got too curious."

Fredrickson said she has no idea why Ruby has been such a terrific therapist. "I know she's on a mission. She has changed people's minds about birds, opened them up to the possibilities of what animals can bring to us. Ruby has shown me that we must never underestimate who animals are—or why they're here."

A disabled canary became an inspiration for scores of crippled children in New Orleans in the early 1900s.

According to a 1902 article in the *New Orleans Times-Democrat*, a Mrs. Sudier raised and studied canaries. "Some time ago she found an afflicted canary which had just come pecked through the shell," the paper said. "The bird had club feet. It could not get around as well as the others, could not swing as gracefully, could not cling to the side of the cage with so much ease, and there was much pathos about the way the little fellow acted.

"The baby canary seemed to realize that there was a difference between himself somehow and the other birds that hopped and fluttered around in their cages with so much ease and grace. But soon the little fellow began to sing, and his singing was a revelation. His throat seemed to have a silver lining, and the notes gurgled out like the laughter of a brook. He was a genius in trilling and twittering after the fashion of his mind.

"Mrs. Sudier soon discovered the rare singing qualities of the little crippled canary, and became more attached to it than ever before. The little fellow became the particular pet of the whole flock. But its owner decided to part with it for a good reason.

"Out in Tulane Avenue there is a little hospital, and it is filled with little children, all of them afflicted in one way or another. . . . The little canary genius, with its club feet, was sent out to the Children's Hospital [where he is] swinging in his awkward way and singing to the crippled children of the institution. Mrs. Sudier thought it would be an object lesson for the little children. . . . He is no doubt a source of great inspiration to them. It is a pretty lesson."

When a distressed duck saw that her babies were in trouble, she did what any good mother would do—she summoned police.

In 2001, Officer Ray Petersen was walking in downtown Vancouver, British Columbia, when a quacking duck tugged at his pants leg. "I looked down and saw this large mallard pulling at my trousers," he told reporters. "She started quacking like mad. I thought it was a bit goofy, so I shoved her away."

The three-pound brown bird scurried over to a storm drain on the side of the street and lay down, but Petersen didn't understand what she wanted. "When I started walking, she ran over and grabbed my pants leg again, then ran back over to the grating," he said.

The officer finally went to investigate and that's when he spotted eight tiny ducklings a few feet under the grate. They apparently had fallen through the gaps. After Petersen called for additional help, two officers arrived with a tow truck. Together, they lifted off the grate and pulled each of the four-inch-long ducklings to safety with a vegetable strainer. Usually mallards are very defensive and will fight humans or animals who get near their offspring, but the mother duck just lay there and watched.

Once the ducklings were safe, the mother duck quickly marched them off to a nearby creek where they jumped into the water and paddled away.

Petersen said, "It's the most amazing thing I've ever seen. This was one really smart bird."

When a mother duck was killed, leaving behind ten tiny orphans, one of the ducklings went for help.

The baby bird left its nine siblings in the pond where they had hatched days earlier, walked up a ramp, waddled across a road and, incredibly, went to the perfect place for help—the nearby RSPCA ambulance base in south London.

RSPCA animal collection officer Barry Gridley told the

Guardian in 2000 he heard a squeaking noise by the front door and came out to see the tiny duckling on the doorstep. He and animal collection supervisor Laura Tutin went to the pond to investigate and found another eight ducklings huddled together on the water. The RSPCA officers fished out the bodies of the mother and one of the babies.

"It is unusual for a duckling to wander off alone because they normally follow each other," said Tutin. "It's as though it said to the other ducklings, 'Don't worry. Stay here while I get some help from the RSPCA office over the road.'" She said without their mother to keep them warm, the ducklings would not have survived the night. "They would have died of hypothermia very quickly if that little one hadn't come to our door."

The mother was believed to have died from a wound to the head.

The ducklings were transferred to the Wandle Valley

Wildlife Hospital where they were found to be in good health. After being kept indoors for about a month, they were put in an outdoor nursery for another three weeks. Then they were returned to the wild.

As for the duckling that saved their lives, it was given a nickname by the staff—Superduck.

By threatening to be a stool pigeon, a pet parrot helped capture three burglars.

According to police in Memphis, Tennessee, the trio ransacked a home one night in 2004 while the occupants were gone. The only one still in the house was Marshmallow, the family's six-year-old green parrot.

At first, the burglars paid no attention to the bird as

they made off with DVD players, computers, radios, TVs, and other electronic gear. But after loading the loot into the getaway car, one of the suspects realized the parrot had heard him using the nickname "JJ"—the moniker of one of the thieves. The bird had started repeating the name.

Fearing that Marshmallow could identify them, the suspects returned to the scene of the crime because they intended to silence the parrot. As the men snatched the would-be informant, which was still in its cage, a neighbor spotted them and called police, who arrived just as the three were speeding away.

During a high-speed chase, the suspects crashed their car a few blocks later into an iron gate. Although the three took off running, police nabbed them and charged them with aggravated burglary and evading arrest. Unfortunately, when the car wrecked, Marshmallow's cage broke. The bird flew the coop and hasn't been seen since.

"They were afraid the bird would 'stool' on them," Major Billy Garrett told the Memphis *Commercial Appeal.* "They actually believed he could identify them."

There was talk on the street that the stool parrot was hiding out in the witness protection program.

Eight stolen cockatiels helped crack a theft ring by whistling the theme song of the old-time comedy team of Laurel and Hardy.

The owner of the birds, who asked not to be named, had his own private aviary in Salisbury, England. In 2003 he purchased his twelfth cockatiel from an acquaintance. "That bird had previously been kept in an indoor cage and its owner had taught it to whistle 'Laurel and Hardy,'" the owner told reporters. The tune, known as "The Ku-Ku Song," was played in most of the Stan Laurel and Oliver Hardy films made in the 1920s, '30s, and '40s. "After I bought the cockatiel and put it in the aviary, soon some of the other birds started to whistle [the tune] as well," the owner said.

It was a good thing they did.

In 2004, a few months after the arrival of the latest cockatiel, four of the man's birds had disappeared. Then a few days later, the rest of his birds were missing along with some other items. It was obvious they had been stolen.

When the owner reported the crime to police, he mentioned that half the flock had picked up the new bird's quirky habit of whistling "The Ku-Ku Song." Police realized that the birds' distinctive whistling could help crack the case. So they issued an appeal through the media, urging members of the public to listen out for birds whistling the Laurel and Hardy tune.

A few days later, police received an anonymous call from someone with an ear for music. He claimed he had heard the unique whistling as he walked past a certain house. Police responded and recovered eight birds and a stolen cage from the address, but the original four birds were still missing. A thirty-three-year-old man and a twenty-seven-year-old woman were arrested on suspicion of theft.

A homing pigeon flew for help when a fishing boat went aground.

In 1936, the Freeport (Long Island) Boatmen's Association established a natural wireless system for fishing boats to communicate with the mainland by using homing pigeons. Many of the locals snickered at the idea, but the first time it was needed, the avian alert system worked.

A charter boat named *Dawn* with fifteen fishermen went aground off the coast. Without a radio, Captain Madison Pearson wrote a short note that said, "Pearson stuck on bar at mouth of Amityville Creek opposite Squaw Island. Advise Coast Guard." He put the note in a canister that he attached to a homing pigeon and released the bird.

The pigeon flew straight to its loft back in Freeport, tripping a wire that rang a bell at the headquarters of the association. One of the members read the note and notified the Coast Guard, which sent out a rescue boat. The crew found the forty-foot fishing boat stuck on a bar where it had drifted after having engine problems. The rescue boat towed the ship off the sandbar and back to the pier.

For several years, the association had forty homing pigeons, two for each of the group's boats. The captain of each boat was allowed to send one bird back with a message about fishing conditions or to get a message relayed to a family member of one of the anglers onboard. One bird was always kept onboard in case of an emergency. The birds were finally phased out when the boats became equipped with two-way radios.

A lost cat was found thanks to an unlikely source—a blue jay.

In 1950, a three-year-old calico named Marquise managed to escape from a veterinarian's office in Ridgewood, New Jersey. It had been staying there while its owners Paul Richard and his wife were on vacation.

When the couple returned home, they learned that their beloved cat had been missing for three weeks. Richard and his friends searched the nearby woods but were unable to find any sign of Marquise. Because the vet's office was twelve miles away from the Richards' home in West Nyack, the searchers began covering a wider area.

Richard had a hunch and returned to the woods near the animal clinic. As the sun began to set, he heard the loud meow of a cat. Excited, he followed the sound, but was disappointed when he discovered it was just a blue jay calling. But then he remembered that jays can mimic sounds, so he followed the bird as it flitted from one tree to another, making a meowing sound.

Feeling more confident that his cat was in the area, Richard then gave a special shrill whistle that he always used to summon Marquise. Sure enough, a few moments later, Marquise scrambled out of a thicket and purred contentedly as it rubbed against Richard's leg. Just then the jay flew off, giving a different call that sounded like a triumphant "Ah! Ha!"

Ruffled Feathers

Beleaguered Birds

A BELOVED RED-TAILED HAWK NAMED PALE MALE and his mate Lola were evicted from their nest on an exclusive Manhattan apartment building, triggering outrage among the city's bird lovers. The brouhaha turned into an ongoing national story—one that eventually had a happy ending.

Pale Male flew into the hearts of New Yorkers in 1991 when he and his mate at the time, First Love, built a love nest on a twelfth-floor cornice of the building, overlooking Central Park on Fifth Avenue and Seventy-fourth Street. Since then, in consort with various female hawks—the latest being Lola—the majestic hawk had spawned about two dozen chicks and remodeled his home until it had grown into a 300-pound, eight-foot-by-three-foot behemoth.

Pale Male—so named because of his unusual whitish plumage—and his family became the darlings of Big Apple bird-watchers, who stood across the street and trained their telescopes and binoculars on the hawks and their nest. Gaining in popularity, Pale Male was the subject of a book, a PBS documentary, and many magazine stories.

But for all the adoration, the hawks had their detractors— their closest neighbors. Residents of the ritzy building hated Pale Male's nasty habit of attacking and devouring local pigeons, rats, and squirrels, then dropping their bloody remains on the sidewalk below by the elegant entrance.

Ruffled Feathers

In 1993 the co-op board had the nest summarily removed. Then Marie Winn, a devoted bird-watcher, intervened on the hawks' behalf. She charged that by destroying the birds' habitat, the board had violated the Migratory Bird Treaty of 1918. She complained to the U.S. Fish and Wildlife Service, which suggested that board members might be embarrassed by the publicity. The board caved in and put back the nest. Pale Male and his family returned.

All seemed fine for the next ten years. But many of the co-op's residents, who included CNN anchorwoman Paula Zahn, were growing irritated by the hawks' practice of bombarding them with droppings and dinner leftovers. Besides, the board's engineer claimed the huge nest was causing the building's facade to crumble.

So the board, headed by Zahn's husband, developer Richard Cohen, once again targeted the birds for eviction. They asked for and received a clarification from the U.S.

Fish and Wildlife Service that said nests of migratory birds may be destroyed when they no longer house live chicks or nesting females. The board quietly voted to remove Pale Male's home. On the afternoon of December 7, 2004, city workers took down the nest and hauled it away.

Booted from their high-rent aerie, the famous lovebirds of prey were now suddenly homeless. When news of the eviction got out, it unleashed a tidal wave of pity and anger. Bird lovers picketed the co-op, brandishing placards recommending, among other things, that passers-by "Honk for Hawks." A demonstrator wearing a hawk costume said, "New York, the nation, and the world love Pale Male and want his nest back."

Fellow protester Tim Laslavic said, "The audacity of what they did here, and the naïveté to believe there wouldn't be an emotional reaction from the people, is ridiculous."

Ben Cosgrove, editor of *Apt. Magazine*, said the hawks

were not "merely symbols of wilderness and freedom; they *are* wilderness and freedom." He added, "They humble us and thrill us, and the fact that of all the places they could have lived, they chose to live here among us, in the heart of the city, somehow makes the destruction of their nest all the more shameful."

The evicted hawks found a temporary new home at an even more posh address. Bird-watchers spotted the pair at the Carlyle Hotel on Madison Avenue and Seventy-sixth Street. The hotel's management announced it would make plans to accommodate them.

Meanwhile, officials of the Audubon Society pressured the co-op board to meet with them. Because of the noisy protests from bird lovers and the intense media attention, the board quickly reached an agreement with the Audubon Society to restore the roost and satisfy safety concerns. An architect designed a stainless-steel cradle complete with spikes to support a new nest for the hawks. The design also included a guardrail that extended beyond the spikes to keep debris from dropping to the street.

Architect Dan Ionescu declined to divulge the cost of the project but said the job presented a unique challenge. "You don't get a call every day asking for a design for a nest for a bird on top of a window of a landmark building," he said. "The birds have been circling and the whole world was watching us, putting on a lot of pressure."

In announcing the agreement, E. J. McAdams, director of the New York City Audubon Society, told a jubilant crowd of fifty bird-watchers, "It's the miracle of Seventy-fourth Street. The grassroots support for Pale Male and Lola has changed the hearts of the building."

Within days, workers began installing a 300-pound, stainless-steel basket above the twelfth-floor cornice of the building, which officials hoped the birds would use as a foundation for a new nest. During the installation, Pale Male soared above Fifth Avenue while Lola initially stayed away from the scene.

But eventually, they settled into their remodeled aerie, built a new nest and became parents again.

"We had an overwhelming response from all over the world," Audubon Society President John Flicker said about the tale of Pale Male. "We had people from Europe, Jordan, Australia, and from all across the country contacting us in an unbelievable outpouring of hope, support, and concern.

"We've pushed nature so far out of our lives, they are living on a little window ledge on Fifth Avenue. And then we almost pushed them off there as well."

A Hawaiian seabird accustomed to warm island breezes picked the wrong yacht to follow. It wound up in frigid Alaska and nearly died from the cold.

The bird, a red-footed booby, began trailing a Kodiak-bound boat as it left Hawaii in 1999. About halfway through the eight-day voyage, the bird plopped on the deck after being battered by a fierce storm. The captain kept the booby in the cabin but the bird grew weaker.

When the yacht docked in Kodiak, the captain contacted the U.S. Fish and Wildlife Service. It arranged to have the booby, which was suffering from severe hypothermia, transferred to Anchorage's Bird Treatment and Learning Center. There, the bird was placed under a heat lamp.

Barbara Doak, rehabilitation director at the center, said that boobies are notorious for following ships. She told the Reuters News Service that she had never seen a warm-weather bird travel so far north. "This one was a young one, and I guess he didn't ask the captain where he was going."

The booby eventually recovered and was returned to Hawaii where presumably it figured the islands were a much better place to live than the glaciers.

A wayward hummingbird that was supposed to be wintering in Mexico was found 3,000 miles away in cold New Jersey.

In November 1996, Pat Turkelson, of Oaklyn, New Jersey, was raking leaves when she bumped into a hummingbird feeder that she had forgotten to take in for the winter. She knew that the tiny birds migrated south by early October. After retrieving the feeder, she left it on her back steps overnight.

"The next morning, my son said, 'There's a hummingbird at the feeder,'" she told the *Philadelphia Inquirer*. "I said, 'Yeah, right.' But there it was."

This wasn't the typical bright green ruby-throated hummingbird that frequents the area in the spring and summer. This hummer was brown with a cream-colored stomach. When it showed up several times a day over the next ten days, Turkelson grew fond of it and named it Turk. But she was worried that it would die as the temperatures dipped.

Not sure what kind of hummingbird it was, she phoned the Audubon Society in Philadelphia. The society posted her sighting on the Internet to its New Jersey members, bringing nearly 200 bird-watchers to her doorstep throughout the following week. They identified the bird as a rufous hummingbird, a species indigenous to the West Coast in the spring and summer and in Mexico in the winter.

"Generally, rufouses aren't here, especially this time of year," said Rachael Soles, clinic supervisor at the Tri-State

Bird Rescue in Newark, Delaware. "They're primarily found in California and the West. This one either got lost or blown off course," she told the newspaper.

Soles, who said her clinic rescued two rufouses a year ago, dispatched a Tri-State volunteer to Turkelson's home. The volunteer brought along the clinic's hummingbird trap—a long, foot-wide tube with food inside and a trapdoor at the end. "We expected to be there a couple of days based on our experience with the birds last year," Soles said. "While our volunteer was setting up, the bird flew right in."

At the clinic, Turk was pronounced a healthy male hummingbird that weighed three grams and was three inches long from tail to beak. Based on its plumage, it was likely anywhere from one to five years old.

As with the previous year's pair, Turk was flown—in a carry-on cage, not in baggage—to a San Diego bird shelter that specializes in hummingbirds.

"The funny thing is," Turkelson told the *Inquirer*, "I've had that feeder up for three years, and in all that time I've never seen a single hummingbird."

A swan that apparently lost its bearings in the dead of night busted through the window of an elderly couple's home and landed in their bed.

Despite suffering deep gashes to its feet and legs, the male cygnet survived.

Jim and Isabel Ballantyne of Renfrewshire, Scotland, were babysitting their six-year-old grandson Ryan in 2004 when the swan made its smashing entrance into their home. The Ballantynes were watching television in the living room when they heard a loud bang followed by breaking

glass. Jim rushed outside to discover their second-floor bedroom window had been shattered.

Meanwhile Isabel ran upstairs to check their room. "I opened the door and shouted to Jim when I saw the bird sitting there," she told the BBC. "It was surrounded by glass and there was blood everywhere."

Jim added, "We both got such a fright, we couldn't believe our eyes at first." He said they were given the "biggest shock of our lives" when they saw the dazed, bleeding swan sitting on their bed.

The couple would normally have been in bed, but because Ryan was over they were still up, said Isabel. "Thank God. I can't imagine what would have happened if it had landed on us. I am absolutely amazed that he survived the smash. I would have thought that he would have broken his neck when he hit the thick glass, but he was fine."

The couple wrapped the dazed bird—which they nick-

named Magoo—in blankets and called the Hessilhead
Wildlife Rescue Trust. When volunteers arrived, they slipped
the swan into a special bag and took it to their center
in Ayrshire.

Founder Gay Christie told reporters that the swan had a
cut on one eye and its feet were bleeding badly. But the wounds
quickly healed and the swan was soon released back into the
wild. Christie thought that the cygnet had lost its bearings
and mistook the upstairs window's reflection for a pond.

A greedy eagle made such a pig of itself that it was
unable to fly.

According to BBC News Online, the bird had overeaten
and was floundering in a snowdrift by the side of the road in

Norway in 2001. It couldn't even fly away when a passing truck driver stopped and tried to help it. The eagle did, however, manage to run off. But Sigbjorn Bjorkedal, a local bird lover, arrived at the scene holding a large sack and chased the bird 600 yards up a mountainside before he finally captured it.

A local ornithologist said it was not unusual for birds of prey to overeat and find themselves grounded until the meal was properly digested. It was estimated that the eagle had consumed a four-and-a-half pound animal.

Bjorkedal took care of the eagle, which appeared to adjust easily to domestic conditions, particularly when it was treated to a hairdryer. "It acted like it had just gone to the hairdresser for a perm," said Bjorkedal. The bird was released into the wild a few days later.

A confused homing pigeon ended up 6,400 miles away from home—and it's not coming back.

In 2002, Vincent McGann, who worked in the office of a diamond mine in South Africa, was startled to see a homing pigeon walk into his office. He could tell it was hungry, so he fed it. Based on the small ring around the bird's leg and stamps on its wing feathers, McGann knew it was a British homing pigeon.

He sent the female bird by courier to Willie Venter, secretary of the South African National Homing Pigeon Organization, in Pretoria. Venter phoned a friend, pigeon fancier John Krug of Liverpool, England, and established within twenty minutes that pigeon GB S82074.99 belonged to a Mr. Sinfield from Derbyshire. Sinfield said the bird—a Jan Aarden, a breed known for being able to fly long distances at high speeds—was a good pigeon that won first place on a 436-mile flight from Brussels, Belgium, to Derbyshire in 2001.

On her ill-fated latest flight in 2002, Sinfield said, the

pigeon was released in Fougeres, France, and was supposed to return to her loft in England. Somewhere along the 321-mile route, she completely lost her way. Sinfield didn't know what had happened to her until he received a call a month later.

Venter said storms over the North Sea could have been the cause. He suspected she flew south for a long distance with a tailwind, and then hitched a ride on a ship farther south. As soon as she saw land, she flew toward it, and because she was so tame, she went begging for food at McGann's office. She picked the right place to visit.

Since it would cost too much to return the pigeon to England, Sinfield said Venter could keep her. Venter decided that her racing days were over and turned her into a breeding pigeon.

A lost racing pigeon took a 7,000-mile round-trip detour when it landed aboard the world's most famous ship, the *Queen Elizabeth 2*.

The misadventure began on June 18, 2001, after owner Ron Horrocks, of North East Lincolnshire, England, packed the pigeon, now nicknamed "QE," on a truck bound for Plymouth with about sixty other birds owned by members of the Wellington Flying Club for a race back to the town of Grimsby. The race—a distance of 281 miles as the pigeon flies—should have taken around six hours at an average flying speed of around 50 mph.

"Because the birds had been kept in their cages in Plymouth for around four days before the race could start due to bad weather, I think he [QE] had become a bit confused," Horrocks told reporters. "He went the wrong way and ended up flying 500 miles out to sea. If he had gone on flying without anywhere to land, he would have just ended up in the water and died."

The wrong-way winged racer was 577 miles off the Irish coast at 7:30 a.m. June 20 when it spotted the QE2, which was on its way to New York from Southampton. With nowhere else to land, the bird perched on the ship's bridge to the amazement of the captain and senior officers. Soon the bird became the number-one celebrity on board.

"The bird was given a perch in the ship's kennels where passengers' pets are usually kept during the voyage," said the ship's captain, Ron Warwick. "He was fed a special menu of corn as we continued across the Atlantic to the USA."

Meanwhile, the QE2's third officer, Grant Hunter, contacted the Royal Pigeon Racing Association (RPRA) by e-mail and reported that the crew had made a perch for the bird and would care for it until they arrived back in Southampton on June 30, 2001.

Karen James of the RPRA was able to determine from

her records that the one-year-old racing pigeon, banded GB 2000B2391, was registered to Horrocks Brothers Loft, of Cleethorpes, North East Lincolnshire, England. At the time the pigeon landed on the *QE2*, it was already 1,102 miles from its home. With ten days left on its ocean voyage, the bird continued on to New York and then returned with the ship to Southampton on June 30 when it was set free.

This time, it didn't get lost. Instead, it made a beeline for its home. Horrocks reported that the seafaring pigeon had returned home by first light on July 1, indicating that the pigeon must have flown directly from Southampton to its home in Cleethorpes, thus completing the final 188 miles of its 7,000-mile round-trip.

"I have a sneaky feeling the bird knew where he was going and just fancied a luxury cruise," James said.

That wasn't the first time a lost racing pigeon hitched a ride aboard the *QE2*.

In June 2000, a British bird missing over the English Channel was discovered getting a lift to New York aboard the luxury liner.

The pigeon, appropriately named Liberty, set off from Nantes, France, four weeks earlier on what was supposed to be a nine-hour, 400-mile homing race back to Derbyshire, England. Caught in fog over the Channel, the three-year-old hen took a wrong turn and settled on the New York-bound liner.

The *QE2* faxed the RPRA to say that it had found and safely captured Liberty along with another racing pigeon from the same race. The two pigeons were apparently sunning themselves on deck when they were discovered. The feathered freeloaders were caught by crewmembers who identified them by their bands. The birds were placed in the liner's kennels for safekeeping.

The RPRA tracked down Vince Webster, owner of one

of the birds. He told reporters he had been raising racing pigeons for thirty-four years, but never had one got so lost. "There are always a few that go astray and get back eventually, but America is a long way to divert," he said.

Liberty earned its name after its ocean-going escapade. "She didn't have a name before, but she must have seen the Statue of Liberty, and it's an appropriate name," Webster said. "She probably thought it would be nicer to have a holiday than come home and go in another race."

A swan crash-landed short of its target and plowed into a bush so hard that it became stuck and couldn't get out. Bird lover Chris Barker of Rochester, Kent, England, was driving home from work when he saw a woman standing by a bush, looking at a large white object. "I stopped and walked up only to find an embarrassed-looking adult mute swan stuck in the middle of a buddleia bush right by the road," Barker wrote in the bird lovers' Web site fatbirder.com. "How long it had been there no one knows as it's a busy road with few people walking down it.

"The bird was truly stuck fast and must have flown low right into the bush. Although there is a small lake nearby, the bird must have mistaken the road for a dike or canal at night, and realized this at the last moment and veered into the medium-sized bush."

There were no apparent injuries to the swan. An RSPCA volunteer had to cut away some of the bush to free the bird and take it away for a checkup.

A porky pigeon was trapped in the chimney of a house for three weeks before the homeowner saved its life—by sucking it out with a vacuum cleaner.

At first Veronica Ingrams, fifty-three, of Bexley, England, didn't know what was causing a fluttering sound in her fireplace in 2002. "I kept hearing this really weird noise, and then I realized I must have a bird stuck up there, although I couldn't see anything," she said.

She called the Bexley Fire Service and the RSPCA, asking them to remove the beleaguered bird. But they were helpless because it was jammed too far up the chimney. She kept waiting and hoping the bird would lose enough weight from not eating and get out on its own.

"The irritating flapping was really wearing me down," said Ingrams, a medical secretary. "Every morning I'd come downstairs and my carpet would be filthy from soot.

Something had to be done."

So, armed with her vacuum cleaner, she opened a small vent in the side of the chimney, thrust the vacuum pipe up into the space, and turned on the machine. Several sooty minutes later, the suction from the vacuum cleaner caught the pigeon, but despite the bird's three-week confinement, it still was too fat to fit through the vent.

So Ingrams called back the Bexley Fire Service. They busted a hole in the side of the chimney and the bird was pulled out safely. The pigeon seemed relatively unfazed by the ordeal and remained at Ingrams' house for several days.

"It seems a bit cruel to use the Hoover on a bird, but it was for the best in the long run," said Ingrams. "The problem now is that I'm left with a big hole in my chimney."

227

Amazing but True Bird Tales

A pet parrot that got stuck in a tree kept swearing at other birds that were trying to attack him.

Rico, a South American parrot, became frightened after a ride on a merry-go-round at a fair in Prince Rupert, British Columbia. The bird flew into the tree and wouldn't come down. Owner Melanie McCarthy tried coaxing her bird, but Rico refused to budge.

McCarthy then summoned the police, the fire department, and the local SPCA for help. They all took turns trying to convince the parrot that it was okay to come down. But Rico wasn't moving from his perch.

"He sat up there for a couple of hours talking away to us, saying 'Come here, come here, go home,'" Melanie told the Canadian Web site canoe.ca. She stayed with Rico all night while two bald eagles kept their eyes on him as a possible snack.

Rico made it safely through the night without any trouble,

but in the morning, several crows launched an attack. Rico fended off the winged assailants by flapping his wings. But it was not until he began uttering a string of nasty expletives that the parrot managed to drive the crows away.

"We usually tell him those are bad words," said McCarthy somewhat sheepishly.

Finally, out of options, McCarthy approved a firefighter's idea to aim a stream of water from a fire hose at Rico in an attempt to force the parrot to flee the tree. "Firefighters hosed him out of the tree, but in full flight, a crow dove on him and grabbed his body just above the tail feathers, just enough to draw blood," McCarthy recalled. Fortunately, Rico flew down and reunited with his owner.

"He was really happy to get home," said McCarthy. "He said 'Hello! Hi!'" He said a few other things, but no swearing. "He's saving those words for any bad birds."

A pet parrot afflicted with vertigo fell out of a tree and broke his leg.

Heights terrified George the parrot and made him get dizzy. So when the bird escaped from his home, his worried owner was surprised and dismayed to see the African gray perched eighty feet up on a tree branch.

In 2002, owner Janet Rose, of Merseyside, England, tried everything to coax the parrot down. Apparently, his fear of heights prevented George from doing anything but stay rooted to the spot. So Rose kept an all-night vigil under the tree, hoping the bird would fly down to her.

He finally reunited with Rose, but not the way she had hoped. After remaining stuck in the tree for over a day, the parrot stepped off the branch—and promptly plunged eighty feet straight to the ground, landing so hard he broke his leg.

"He is awake and looking at us, although he hasn't said anything yet," Rose told the *Liverpool Daily Post* the day after the incident. "George is like a baby to me. He sits at the table with us every Sunday at dinnertime, and I make Yorkshire pudding especially for him. He has his own placemat at the table. He is one of the family."

George soon recovered, but never perched on anything taller than a rose bush.

A robin took an unintended ride in a car—actually, in the hood of a car.

Ken Johnston, of Philadelphia, was driving his 1968 Dodge Coronet one morning in 1978 when he noticed a robin flying perpendicular to the path of the car. "We reached the same point in space at exactly the same time," he recalled in the chatline Birdchat. "I looked to the side and the robin wasn't there, nor was he in the road. It was as though it disappeared into thin air."

About four hours later, Johnston stopped for gas at the local station. "When I popped the hood to check the oil, the robin flew out from the area between the grille and the radiator and scared the daylights out of me," Johnston recalled. "Guess he enjoyed all the bugs coming through the grille!"

A parrot that lost its beak in a fight avoided starving to death thanks to a diet of Kentucky Fried Chicken dinners and vanilla ice cream.

Missy, a nine-year-old Corella parrot at Nelson's Natureland Zoo in New Zealand, lost its bottom beak in a fight with its partner Bert in 2002. Reconstructive surgery failed, causing Missy's keepers to fear that the bird would starve to death.

Zoo spokeswoman Gail Sutton told the *Nelson Mail* that Missy lost a third of its body weight after the attack. "It was touch and go for a long time, but she's doing really well now and doesn't seem too traumatized by it all," said Sutton. "I think she prefers her new diet to seed anyway, and she absolutely loves chips. They're her favorite."

Missy had to relearn the basics of eating and now uses her remaining beak as a type of scoop. Her top beak was also fractured in the attack but was glued back together. She lives alone because keepers don't want to risk her being attacked again.

An avian apartment complex built by wild parakeets became too popular and finally collapsed under the weight of all the birds' nests.

The "founders" of the compound were a pair of monk parakeets that had escaped from captivity in 1979 and settled in an abandoned factory chimney in Ukkel, Belgium. It was such a comfy place that over time more than sixty birds made their homes in the chimney. In fact, they built so many nests to accommodate the breeding birds that the colony measured nearly twenty feet high.

The newspaper *Het Nieuwsblad* reported that people living near the empty factory loved the parakeets and had asked the company to leave the chimney intact after the plant had relocated. The company agreed.

But the weight of all those nests combined with the erosion of the old chimney caused everything to come crashing to the ground in 2002.

"Monk parakeets like to breed in colonies," explained Jan Rodts, director of the Bird Protection Association of Flanders. "Each year they built a new nest above the old one. After all these years they had built a huge apartment block."

Rodts spoke to the newspaper immediately after the chimney collapsed. He said, "Although the sixty birds are now homeless, a real disaster has been prevented. They have not laid eggs yet and probably won't because they have no time to build new nests."

An endangered macaw, being illegally imported into Canada, managed to save itself by screaming from inside a smuggler's briefcase as the man was trying to clear customs.

According to canada.com, the smuggler was almost through customs at Ottawa International Airport when the bird started making a noise. The squawking—described by witnesses as "more of a desperate scream"—caught the attention of a customs officer. Meanwhile, the would-be importer gave the briefcase a shake and tried to shuffle to another line. Officers seized the man's briefcase, which he'd carried on a flight from Florida to Ottawa, and freed the bird, which witnesses described as "ruffled."

The forty-eight-year-old smuggler pleaded guilty to charges of unlawfully importing a rare bird without a license. He was fined $1,500, and the macaw, whose species lives in the tropical rainforests of Central and South America, was taken to a rare bird center.

On a Lark

Caring and Crazy Birders

AN INJURED OWL OWES ITS SIGHT to some bird lovers.

State-licensed wildlife rehabilitator Donna Fletcher of Plattsburgh, Pennsylvania, picked up a wild barred owl that had been injured in 1999. When she examined it, she discovered it had a detached retina caused by blunt trauma to the head. She knew there was no way this bird of prey could survive out in the wild—at least not without laser eye surgery.

So Fletcher called local ophthalmologist Dr. Kjell Dahlen, who specialized in cataract surgery, but on people, not animals. "I thought there was nothing I could do," Dahlen told the *Plattsburgh Press-Republican*. But he was impressed by Fletcher's compassion and, after doing a little research on the anatomy of the eye of an owl, decided to give it a shot.

Fletcher brought in the owl, which she named K.D. after the doctor's initials. The bird proved easier to work on than he'd expected, Dahlen told the paper. Because a barred owl's eye is similar in size to a human's, the surgical equipment was compatible. Also, an owl's eye doesn't move—the bird turns its head to see—so by simply immobilizing its head, its eye couldn't shift position.

During the operation, Fletcher held the feathered patient immobile while Dahlen used his laser beam to mend the sight-threatening tear. Dahlen's first owl operation was a success. The retina was reattached.

Fletcher kept the owl until it recovered and could show that it hadn't lost any of its hunting skills. Then she and assistant rehabilitator Rodney LaValley set it free while Dahlen and his family proudly looked on.

"It's rewarding," Dahlen said. "Owls are very beautiful animals."

Since K.D.'s successful return to the wild, Dahlen has performed the same surgery on several birds. According to the paper, his laser surgery has saved the vision of three of four owls.

A framed photograph of K.D. hangs on the wall at Dahlen's practice, Eye Care for the Adirondacks. The ophthalmologist said he likes to think the owl is still swooping through the night air, its keen night vision scanning the ground for prey.

A great horned owl named Minerva can see clearly, thanks to concerned bird lovers. Veterinarians say she's the only wild bird in the world with surgically implanted artificial lenses.

In December 2003, Renee Prausa called veterinarian Dr. Chris Katz in Two Rivers, Wisconsin, to ask if it was normal for an owl to sit on a fence for three days without moving. After Katz explained that such lethargy was a real danger sign, especially in such a cold climate, Prausa contacted the rescue group Wildlife of Wisconsin (WOW).

Susan Theys, a full-time volunteer for the rescue organization, picked up the female bird. "She was so weak and dehydrated we had to put a tube into her stomach," she told CNN. But even though she was weak and couldn't see much, the owl tried to fend off her rescuers by using her talons. Other than suffering from malnutrition and cataracts in both eyes, which prevented her from catching prey, the one-year-old owl was healthy.

So WOW volunteers decided to rehabilitate the bird and brought her to the University of Wisconsin Veterinary School in Madison. The staff there named her Minerva, after the ancient goddess of war and wisdom. "She's a really tough bird; she fit both the war and wisdom descriptions," Dr. Renee Carter, a resident in veterinary ophthalmology, told CNN.

Dr. Chris Murphy, professor of ophthalmology at the veterinary school, led the surgical team in a four-hour procedure that removed both cataracts and implanted artificial lenses so the owl could again see things in focus. Murphy said an owl's eyes are adapted for nocturnal hunting. "There's a big pupil and a big cornea to collect a lot of light," Dr. Murphy explained. "Even though owls only weigh about two kilograms [4.4 pounds] their eyes are significantly bigger than a human's."

Drs. Murphy, Carter, and Katie Diehl donated their

services for the surgery. Wildlife of Wisconsin paid $300 for anesthesia and other drugs.

Dr. Carter said the experience with this owl will help in understanding and designing lenses for other birds, possibly endangered species such as condors and eagles.

After her eyes healed and Minerva proved she could see and catch live prey in a confined area, it was time to let her go. She was fitted with a radio transmitter so her movements could be tracked, and released at the same place where she had been rescued in eastern Wisconsin.

"It's always gratifying to release an animal," WOW's Jerry Theys told CNN. "This one may be special because it took a lot of people to get this bird on her way."

A maker of artificial limbs provided a peg leg for a peregrine falcon and saved the bird's love life.

In 1999, a birder captured a falcon whose leg had to be amputated because the bird had been injured in a pole trap. The falcon was taken to the New Forest Owl Sanctuary in England where it was given the name Bracken and nursed back to health.

A chance conversation in a pub with a friend who walked on two artificial legs led sanctuary owner Bruce Berry to visit Bob Watts, managing director of Dorset Orthopaedic. Berry asked him if he could create an artificial leg for the bird. Watts replied there was no reason why a tiny prosthetic couldn't be made for Bracken. After making a plaster mold, Watts constructed a silicon leg, which slipped onto the falcon's stump like a shoe.

"Because it's a female, it needs the leg for breeding," Berry told the BBC. "Without the foot, it can't balance and it needs to balance to be able to mate." With her new artificial limb, Bracken was soon enjoying her love life.

A bald eagle with its beak almost completely shot off had reconstructive surgery thanks to a local dentist.

The bird was found in 2002 near the town of Tofino on Vancouver Island, British Columbia, by passers-by who wrapped it in a blanket and brought it to a wildlife preserve.

"The whole top of his beak was shot away, right to the front of his forehead, so it left him with the tip of his beak and his hard palate," Dr. Brian Andrews told CBC Radio. "Sort of like someone took a rifle and shot you through the face, left the tip of your nose and your teeth and tore all your sinuses out."

The bird could eat only little bits of food and needed two months to recuperate from the trauma of being shot. In its condition, it could have never survived in the wild. So volunteers at the preserve asked Andrews, a dentist in the nearby town of Nanaimo, if he could give the eagle a beak job.

Dr. Andrews and his technician created an artificial beak molded from the same acrylic material that athletic mouth guards are made of and modeled after a picture from the cover of a *National Geographic* magazine. He made the beak with airholes and even stained it yellow to make it look as natural as possible. It was attached with a stainless-steel rivet.

Within a few weeks, the eighteen-pound bald eagle was ripping bits of salmon to pieces again with his new beak. But he was not allowed to return to the wild.

In honor of the dentist who donated his services, the preserve volunteers named the bald eagle Brian.

Northern Ireland Water Service employee Terry McHale hung up the keys of his truck for several weeks in 2004 so a mother bird could tend to her fledglings in their nest—in the vehicle's gearbox by the driver's seat.

McHale and his colleagues noticed a pied wagtail flying in and out of the open window of the utility's tow truck parked in their depot yard in Londonderry. After a long search, they came across the nest hidden next to the gearbox in the cab, but they didn't think the mother would hatch her eggs there.

Although he didn't touch the empty nest, McHale drove the truck on several trips before realizing that the mama bird was tailing him all the way.

Workers at the depot noticed that when the truck was parked, the bird kept bobbing in and out of the vehicle. "Every time I went out, she started following me in and out of the yard," McHale told BBC News Online. "The mother was going mad. After I would come back, she would be waiting and hop on to the vehicle while I was reversing."

Despite all the long journeys, the mother did get her hatching act into gear and laid three eggs. One morning, McHale discovered that the eggs had cracked open and three baby chicks were sitting at third gear.

After contacting the RSPB, McHale immediately decided not to drive the vehicle. He let it sit in the depot yard for three weeks to allow the new family a little space. He did not start up the truck again until the birds could fly off on their own. "I believe that every animal should have a wee chance in life," he said.

For his compassion and concern for the birds, the Animal Welfare Federation and the RSPB honored McHale with a merit award and also gave one to the water service for supporting his decision not to drive the truck.

Representative Norman McCombe from the RSPB said, "At a time when reports of incidents involving cruelty to animals are all too common, it makes a welcome change to come across a story of care and compassion for wildlife by a public service employee who was fully supported by his management."

On a Lark

Four Belgian bird lovers bought part of a farmer's crop so that a pair of rarely seen buzzards could rear their chicks safe from the hazards of a combine.

In the summer of 1999, the amateur ornithologists were delighted to discover that the buzzards—a type not seen in Belgium in more than twenty years—had made a nest on the ground in a wheat field near Brussels. The newspaper *Le Soir* said the bird lovers were worried that the two chicks would not have learned how to fly by the time harvesting began. So the four paid the farmer 17,000 Belgian francs ($442) for 5,000-square yards of the crop surrounding the nest. That way, they were able to ensure that the combine wouldn't come close to the nest.

Their plan worked. Soon after the harvesting season, the chicks had been safely reared and flew off.

A robin rescued after it was grounded from a bad snow-storm finally flew to sunny Florida for the winter—aboard a passenger jet.

The bird was weak, disoriented, and unable to fly when it was found by Michael Reynolds in the snowy countryside of Addison, Maine, in 1973. He brought the robin to bird lover Elizabeth Parrington, who kept it alive on a diet of worms and sliced apples. She named the bird Flip and kept it in a cage in her house located on a farm outside Addison.

"It makes me feel sad to see wild things confined, but what can I or anyone do?" Parrington told the Associated Press at the time. "The poor thing would die of hunger or the cold outside."

As Flip's health improved, its rescuers wondered how

long it should be confined within a cage. Parrington thought about allowing Flip to use her Christmas tree to perch. But she knew she had to figure out a way to get the bird to a warmer climate where its brethren had migrated for the winter.

Luckily, she learned that friends Mr. and Mrs. Raymond Joy were planning to fly to Jacksonville, Florida. Since they were also bird lovers, they agreed to escort Flip to Florida and release the robin there.

Parrington built a mini mobile home with a cardboard box, screening, and scraps of wood to hold Flip during the trip south. She also put in a supply of the bird's favorite food—worms and apples. Flip flew—but not in the conventional way like his fellow robins—with the Joys to Jacksonville. There, Flip was released, no doubt feeling the warmth of the Florida sun as well as the TLC of some Maine bird lovers.

The mayor of Portland, Maine, was forced out of office—by a pigeon. But the city's leader didn't mind being unseated because it was for a good cause.

In 2001, a pigeon flew into Mayor Cheryl Leeman's office over the weekend through an open window at Portland City Hall. The pigeon, one of many that congregate on the building's granite sills and make a mess of its giant clock tower, then built a nest under the mayor's desk and laid an egg.

The bird flew away when custodian Orrin Bimpson showed up Monday to clean the second-floor office. Bimpson spotted a nest of twigs with a single white egg beneath the mayor's desk. He informed Leeman, who asked that the office window be kept open so the pigeon could return to the nest. On Tuesday, Bimpson discovered the pigeon was back, and a second egg was in the nest.

After officials were told not to disturb the bird while it tended to its eggs, the mayor moved out of her office. Pigeon expert Gil Levasseur said that trying to move the nest would only kill off the baby birds because the mother would keep returning to the original spot and not look anywhere else.

"People are always accusing me of hatching something," Mayor Leeman quipped to the Associated Press. The mayor said she just wanted to do what was right. "I always take care of my constituents, regardless of who or, in this case, what they are."

But just because the mayor was understanding didn't mean that city officials love pigeons. The truth is they wish the birds would perch somewhere else. In fact, in 2004 city hall installed loudspeakers blaring electronic squeals that sound like birds of prey to ward off the pigeons. A $500 solar-powered machine shrieks all day and runs on stored solar power at night when most pigeons visit the front steps. It did little to deter the birds.

Russian President Vladimir Putin came to the rescue of an injured seagull that he found on the grounds of his vacation home in 2004.

The country's Center TV reported that Putin discovered the stricken bird during a short break at his Bocharev Ruchey country residence in the popular Black Sea resort of Sochi. One of the gull's wings was broken, so the president ordered that the bird be taken to a local bird sanctuary. No one knew how the gull had broken its wing.

"Quite how the bird made it into grounds of the high-security presidential dacha is a mystery," the TV report said. "But it got lucky. The president decided to look after it. Any Olympic champion would be jealous of the attention that was lavished on this bird."

The gull recovered at the sanctuary, but the damage to its wing meant it never would be able to return to the wild.

A species of a rare stork was on the verge of becoming extinct because of the high mortality rate of its hatchlings. But then conservationists came up with a clever—and low-cost—way to save baby storks.

There are only about 1,000 greater adjutant storks left in the world, and about 80 percent of them live in the Indian state of Assam. These storks build their nests high on the limbs of the majestic silk cotton tree in the remote forests of northeastern India. But in recent years, according to *National Geographic News*, a growing number of hatchlings had been falling out of the nests. If the sixty-five-foot to 100-foot fall didn't kill the baby birds, their injuries left them as easy prey for dogs and crows.

Scientists were afraid the death toll from plunging out of nests could seriously impair the species' battle against extinction. So in 2002, conservationists began stringing up safety nets around trees that held stork nests. The plan seems to be working because the death toll from falls has dramatically decreased.

Amazing but True Bird Tales

A flock of wild birds seemed happy that a bird lover fed them after a major snowfall, but they complained about the slow service, according to the online newsletter *Critterchat*.

After a thirty-two-inch snowfall, Jean Robinson of Ambler, Pennsylvania, was snowbound and unable to stock the bird feeders as usual. The best she could do was put some food out on a piece of paneling, which she laid on top of the snow in her backyard. The birds devoured the food.

At 6 a.m. the following morning, Robinson was awakened by a loud rapping on the patio door and rushed to see if a neighbor needed help. Instead, she discovered a large and impatient crow looking for more food. Behind the bold spokesbird stood a motley crowd of hungry birds waiting to be served at their makeshift table. She fed them as quickly as she could.

The demanding customers—led by the bold crow— returned to wake her up at 6 a.m. for the next three days.

On a Lark

A bird lover was passing by St. Michael's Church in Bath, England, in 2002 when he noticed an owl seemed to be in trouble in the belfry. He immediately phoned the RSPCA to report the stricken bird, but after an inspector from the animal charity arrived to help, he called off an operation to rescue the bird.

That's because the owl was stuffed.

It had been placed on the belfry a few years earlier by the owners of a nearby camera and binocular shop. "We put the owl up there so our customers could have something appropriate to look at before they make a purchase," explained Robin Gower, from Ace Optic. "It also scares the pigeons away from the belfry of the church."

In a typical British understatement, Janet Kipling,

spokeswoman for the RSPCA, said, "The inspector con-
cluded it did not need rescuing."

Trying to be a conscientious bird lover became a big
headache for Mike Madden.

In 2001, the forty-eight-year-old welder grew concerned
about dwindling food supplies for the birds around his cottage
in Huddersfield, England. So he turned himself into a walking
bird table. That's right, a bird table.

According to the *Manchester Guardian*, Madden designed
a table that fit on top of his head. He filled it with nuts, and
set out for a field test in the woods with his friend Craig
Bailey. But after a few paces, the quiet forest air was shattered

by a kaboomlike sound. The table broke into pieces as Madden collapsed on the ground in agony with whiplash. A large gray squirrel, its mouth full of nuts, fled the scene and ran into the bushes.

The following day, Madden, who was full of painkillers and had his neck in a brace, told the paper, "I didn't see much. But Craig told me he saw the squirrel fly through the air and land on my head. I have always liked squirrels. But once you've had one land on your head at about thirty miles an hour, you can easily go off them."

British bird lover Neil Symmons was proud that he had established an ongoing relationship with a tawny owl.

Every evening at dusk, he would go out into his garden and imitate the owl's calls. And most every time, he would hear an answer from the wild.

One day in 1997, Symmons' wife Kim mentioned her husband's nocturnal pastime to their neighbor Wendy Cornes. Wendy thought that was interesting because, she said, her husband Fred was also spending his evenings calling to an owl and getting a response. Only then did the men realize that their feathered friend was really human and living next door.

"I felt like such a twit," Neil told the *Daily Mail* newspaper from his home in southwestern England.

Fred, his chagrined neighbor, said, "I never dreamed I was fooling my neighbor, who was fooling me."